The Police Control
of the Slave
in South Carolina

Howell Meadors Henry
(1879-1956)

Originally published
1914

Contents

PREFACE

IN THE FALL of 1909 the late Professor Frederick W. Moore suggested to me as a topic for investigation, the police control of the negro in the period of 1861-1865 and following years. It was his suggestion that by using several states as illustrations I should show to what extent the Southern people sought to perpetuate not slavery, but the same method of controlling the emancipated negro which was in force under the slavery regime, the difficulties which were met with from without and the measure of success attained. The first question arising was: what was that method? It was soon evident that the laws on the statute books did not adequately answer the question. To get a clear understanding of that system another question, or two other questions, had to be answered: to what extent were these laws enforced; and, what extra-legal method may have been resorted to in a system so flexible as slavery was? These questions caused the monograph to assume large proportions; for in only a few of the states has the history of slavery been written. Beginning in South Carolina, my native state, I soon became attracted by the possibilities of a study of the institution of slavery from this point of view of slave control in one of the oldest communities. Hence in order to bring this within the compass of a doctoral dissertation, at the later suggestion of Professor Sioussat, I limited the study to one state and to a study of the ante-bellum period, attempting, as far as possible, to show to what extent the laws were enforced. It is my hope, at some later time, to be able, with this study as a basis, to answer the original question as it affects South Carolina.

It affords me pleasure to acknowledge assistance in the way of helpful suggestions and criticism from Professors Sioussat, Dyer and Mims of the Vanderbilt Faculty; Professor U. B. Phillips, of the University of Michigan, and T. D. Jervey, Esq., of Charleston. To Miss Fitz Simmons and her assistants at the Charleston Library; Miss Webber, of the South Carolina Historical Society; A. S. Salley, Jr., of the South Carolina

Historical Commission; Miss Rion, of the South Carolina University Library; and the County Clerks of Court of several counties in the State, I am indebted for assistance in collecting materials. To these and others who have lent me aid I wish to take this opportunity of expressing my appreciation.

H. M. HENRY.

Vanderbilt University

Nashville, Tenn., April 1, 1913.

CHAPTER I. Introductory Sketch

South Carolina is situated between 32° and 36° north latitude, and 78° and 84° longitude west of Greenwich. The "fall line" extends from near North Augusta on the Savannah River in a straight line to Columbia and thence to the North Carolina boundary near the place where the Great Peedee enters the state. The portion of the state north of this line with its rapidly running rivulets, rolling, rocky and often sterile hills, red with iron deposits, is known as the "up country." The northwestern corner of the state, crossed by a part of the Allegheny range, is decidedly mountainous. Below the fall line are often found considerable tracts of sandy, barren land covered in places with shrubbery, broken occasionally by strips of fine farming land. Extending toward the eastern corner is some of the best cotton producing soil in the state. Going further toward the south the rivers become sluggish and trespass on the bottom lands forming extensive swamps with a tendency to malaria, a condition more or less continuous until the coast is reached.

The first permanent settlement was made near Charleston in 1670. The government was administered by the Proprietors, to whom the territory had been granted by the king, until 1719, when owing to continual disagreement between the Proprietors and the settlers the colony was made a Royal Province. Until about the middle of the eighteenth century, when a treaty was made with the Indians by which land concessions were obtained, there were no settlements in the upper part of the state other than mere trading posts. South Carolinians took a prominent part in the revolutionary movements of 1776 and later; and after the conflict their leaders participated very largely in the affairs of the young nation. The Federalist leaders in South Carolina toward the close of the century had to give way before the rise of the Republican party. A new generation of statesmen with leaders like Lowndes and Calhoun soon took an influential part in national politics involving the issues arising in the war of 1812 and the country's growth after that conflict. Later, however, the disagreements over the tariff leading up to the Nullification troubles caused the state to lose prestige in Congress. Under the leadership of Calhoun, who in a sense represented the slavery interests of the South, the attitude of the state until 1860 became one of distrust of the federal government, and from a place of prominence in the councils of the nation she pursued a policy of resistance all her own which finally culminated in secession in 1860.

Now we turn to the economic life of the people. Considerable time was spent by the colonists in experimenting with crops to find one sufficiently profitable to render the colony self-supporting. Rice, it was soon discovered, could be grown to advantage and for a century it remained the most important crop. Indigo growing also, thanks to the experiment of Eliza Lucas, came to be a profitable industry owing to the encouragement it received from bounties of the British government. These bounties ceased with the breaking out of the Revolution, after which the indigo industry waned. But not until the invention of the cotton gin toward the close of the eighteenth century did the state come to have a staple crop greatly in demand and at the same time one almost uniformly adapted to the soil in practically all sections. It had been observed that none but negro labor could flourish in the low swampy country. This fact had given impetus to the importation of African slaves before the up-country was opened to settlement. It was soon discovered after the stimulation given cotton culture by the invention of a machine to separate the seed from the lint that slave labor could be used to greatest advantage in cotton growing. This discovery determined the economic policy of the state and fastened slavery upon its social organization. This was true of the up-country as well as of the low-country and gradually made the state a unit in its policy with reference to slavery.

As we have seen, slavery had acquired a strong foothold in the state before the cotton industry became prominent. Not only the need of cheap labor, but the cupidity of the English slave trader was a contributing cause to the growth of slavery. This slave trade to America was protected by the English government often in the face of protests made by the colonies. Slaves were first introduced into the colony from the Barbadoes in 1671 by Sir John Yeamans. The number grew from year to year both by increase of the native born and by importations until in 1708 it is estimated to have been 4,100. Within about a quarter of a century the number is estimated to have been, in 1735, 40,000. It is probable that at the outbreak of the Revolutionary war the number had reached nearly 100,000. According to the first federal census of 1790 the number of slaves in the state was 108,805. The colored population increased steadily in an almost uniform ratio until 1860, the official enumeration of that year being: slaves, 402,406; free colored, 9,914, or a total of 412,320 negroes in the state. A few figures as to their distribution will be interesting. Hammond says that in 1790 the "upper and middle regions" of South Carolina had only about 28,000 slaves out of a total for the state of 108,805. Schaper for the purposes of his study of sectionalism in the state deduces the following interesting figures from the census of 1860: there were 26,701 slave owners in the state with an average of fifteen slaves to each owner; the average per owner in the low country was twenty-one, while in the up-country it was eleven; the largest plantation was in Georgetown with one thousand slaves; seven plantations employed five hundred slaves each; twenty-two had three hundred each. He estimates that there were 26,701 households interested in slavery as against 31,559 households not so interested.

McCrady has shown very conclusively the influence of the Barbadian slave code upon the Carolina code of 1712. Both had identical preambles. A comparison of some of the provisions of the two codes reveal further similarities in the following particulars: no white person was to suffer punishment for injuring or killing a slave who resisted lawful chastisement; at first only a fine was imposed upon a white person for the murder of a negro, although later, as in South Carolina, the penalty was made death; the slave was denied the right of self-defense against a white person; negro evidence against a white person was not accepted in any court; mutilation and other graduated punishments were provided for slaves; the court for the trial of slaves was composed of magistrates and freeholders, though a unanimous verdict was necessary for conviction of a capital offense, which was not the case in South Carolina. It is no more than a fair conclusion that the code of the English Barbadoes was the basis of the Carolina code.

J. C. Ballagh, who in his History of Slavery in Virginia has elaborated the legal phase of slavery, thinks it is difficult to say how far Spanish slavery in America influenced English slavery, but probably if there was any influence at all it was very slight. This suggests another inquiry to which the following pages will revert: to what extent can these American codes be traced, if at all, to the ancient slavery of the Greeks and Romans? Of this Ballagh says that it is "one of institutional similarity rather than causal relation." It was after the system was a realized fact that writers and jurists turned to the institutions of decayed civilizations for comparisons and authority.

But if we turn to the system of indented servitude we probably get the germ idea of the laws for slave control. The white redemptioner was sold for a term of service along with the slave, the chief difference between his status and that of the slave being that the former labored under an indenture for a limited time, the latter under an indenture for life. The laws prevented the indented servant from buying or selling by providing punishment for any person who traded with him; he was not allowed to leave the master's premises without permission; an offense against a servant was not so heavily punished as one against a freeman; he was subject to correction with moderate chastisement by the master; when he ran away his term of service was lengthened on his re-capture; he received from the master a certificate of freedom at the end of his term of servitude. The term of service in the case of the indented servant was limited, in that of the slave it was for life,—this contrast marks the point of departure in dealing with an indented servant and in dealing with a slave; the latter was serving a term for life, hence corporal punishment as a penalty was resorted to more freely. This view led to the more general idea, that the master ought to be given complete control over the slave, with some limitations, of course. The earliest preserved laws of the colony show little or no distinction between the white servant and the black slave as to control and management. But the number of slaves increased so rapidly and their barbaric character was so pronounced that a more comprehensive policy had to be sought. The regulations which were sufficient for a small number of white servants, indented for a limited period of time, were found to be quite inadequate for the large number of blacks owned absolutely by the white man. Here the differentiation seems to have begun, and so at about this stage of development the government turned to the English plantation system of the West Indies for suggestions which took form in the Carolina slave code.

The system of control as we know it during the last half century of the existence of slavery in the South is clearly a development from conditions arising out of the presence in the colony of the African negroes with barbaric traits. These laws were amended and added to as the needs of the master required from time to time, and as the necessity for peace and good order in the community seemed to demand. A few acts were passed before 1712 but it was in that year that the first elaborate law for the control of the slaves was enacted. This act was completely revised and replaced by a more comprehensive law passed in 1740, commonly known as the Negro Law. This law of 1740 was re-enacted after the Revolutionary war, and until 1860, though amended, remained the organic black code. Other amendatory acts were passed from time to time but the law of 1740 remained the basis of all later slave regulation

6

CHAPTER II. Legal Status of the Slave

After some method had come to be applied in the control and management of the blacks the courts began to interpret the system of slavery and the relations of the master to his slave, and to give some fixed legal form to the institution. It may be observed at the outset that the decisions of the courts are along the lines of expediency and that no fine-spun theory interfered with the early established practical management of the slave. The court for the most part defines what the codes and customs developed into laws are, enforcing its mandates of humanity toward the ward and encouraging in a conservative way all philanthropic movements toward a more liberal interpretation of the institution.

Of the general control of the black population in the ante-bellum South Professor Phillips says in substance that they were controlled more by men than by laws; that the statutes were placed on the books chiefly for emergency use, but under ordinary circumstances many of them were dead letters. This seems to be the correct view. For example, the law to prohibit trading with a slave without permission from the master was very stringent and often vigorously enforced when the trading was done by persons who deliberately undertook to gain advantage by the theft of the slave. When, however, the slave was selling his own produce with the permission of his master bargains were openly made and no complaint arose. On the other hand the Seamen Acts, prohibiting the presence of free negroes openly at the ports when they were members of crews of visiting ships, were apparently always enforced to the letter. The subject then presents the difficulty of determining to what extent the laws were carried out.

The Act of 1712 declared that all negroes, mulattoes and mustizoes who had "been sold, or now are held or taken to be, or hereafter shall be bought or sold for slaves, are hereby declared slaves" together with their children. The determination of the condition of the child as to slavery or freedom was made to depend upon the status of the child's mother. Slaves were in this act defined as "in the law to be chattels personal in the hands of their owner." There must have been, even at that time, a considerable number of free negroes and it does not appear that public sentiment tolerated any effort to reduce a free person of color to slavery when his title to freedom was unquestionable. This act further provided that in case any negro claimed to be held unjustly in slavery when he had the right to freedom any white person could apply to the courts in his behalf and secure appointment as guardian, and after entering into bond guaranteeing to produce the negro whenever the court might demand him, have a hearing on the merits of the case, the burden of proof resting with the plaintiff. If the negro should be declared entitled to the right of freedom the defendants were to be held for the costs of the trial. But if the defendant should win the suit the court might inflict such punishment upon the negro "not extending to life or limb as in the opinion of the court is fit." Thus it would seem that the difficulties were great even where a negro had a good case. Having no legal standing in the courts he must secure as his guardian some interested white person; and he must then prove his right to freedom, though himself disqualified as a witness, while the defense was under no obligation to offer testimony; and corporal punishment, which if ordered by the court in case of the failure of his contention, probably awaited him at the hands of the master whose claim had been questioned—all of which he was doubtless made aware. These hindrances doubtless prevented all but the clearest cases, and those demanded by the sentiments of humanity, from coming to the courts at all. It was probably intended to reach only cases of free negroes who had been kidnapped and sold into slavery.

There were some such cases tried. One that is left on record is that of Miller vs. Reigne heard by the Court of Appeals in 1835. The court set free two colored women whom it declared to have been wrongfully held in slavery. The evidence on which the court reached its decision was that they had been acting as free persons for more than twenty years, and that this presumed a deed of manumission prior to 1820.

The question occasionally arose as to the proportion of negro blood required to constitute a negro in the eyes of the law. This is important, for if determined a negro, the person is not entitled to jury trial nor is he capable of giving evidence in court against a white person.

Judge O'Neall, for many years a justice of the highest court, in his manual, "The Negro Law in South Carolina," if after stating that no specific rule had been laid down, says that it is a question for the jury, but indicates that if it is made to appear that if the person has less than one-eighth of negro blood in his veins the jury ought to find him white, and if more than one-fourth they "must find him a negro." The Court of Appeals had been called upon before this to determine the matter but went no further than to say that the court may determine by inspection of features or reputation as to amount of negro blood and also as to whether he had been received in society as a white person.

The sessions record of Kershaw district for the fall term of 1845 contains the following:

In the Matter of Wm. Scott.

Jury No. 2 tried this case and returned the following verdict: We find the relator, Wm. Scott, to be a free negro, mulatto or mustizo.

Foreman.

This verdict must have been set aside—though the record does not show it—or there was another "Wm. Scott," for on April 6, 1847, he was found guilty of assault and battery on a slave, and on April 8 sentenced to one month's imprisonment. At the spring term in 1846 it appears that the question of the color of four persons was submitted to a jury, probably to determine whether or not they had standing in the session court, and they were officially found to be mulattoes. The sessions record of Marlborough district for 1850 notes that an indictment handed to the grand jury was returned with the following endorsement signed by the foreman:

"We report him a free person of color." But from what sources shall an interpretation of this new relation of whites and blacks to each other be had? The slave was not a chattel in the same sense that a lower animal was a chattel, but a person, in a limited legal sense it is true; he did not enjoy the rights of equality with the white man, nor did he enjoy the same rights before the law. In a few cases the Court of Appeals undertook to answer the fundamental questions as to the legal status of the slave which might arise. In 1812 in the case of the Executors of Walker vs. Bostick & Walker it was pointed out that the Roman Law and not the English Common Law was to be the guide and source of authority in interpreting the slave laws. The court said in part:

"The condition of slaves in this country is analogous to that of the slaves of the ancients, the Greeks and Romans and not that of the villeins of feudal times. They are, generally speaking, not considered as persons but as things. Almost all our statute regulations follow the principles of the civil law in relation to slaves except in a few cases, wherein the manners of modern times softened by the benign principles of Christianity could not tolerate the severity of the Roman regulations. But in most other respects they are considered as property." Again in 1835 the court had occasion to say:

"The status, the entire civil and political condition of the villein, was in almost every particular different from that of our slave. He had a perfect civil and political capacity and all the rights of a freeman against every person but his lord; and with respect to the lord was very different from that of the slave."

As to the slave's rights under the common law the Constitutional Court in 1818 said if

"The peace of society and the safety of individuals required that slaves should be subjected to the authority and control of all freemen when not under the immediate authority of their masters." And again in 1847:

"A slave can invoke neither Magna Charta nor common law.... In the very nature of things he is subject to despotism. Law to him is only a compact between his rulers, and the questions which concern him are matters agitated between them. The various acts concerning slaves contemplates throughout the subordination of the servile class to every free white person and enforce the stern policy which the relation of master and slave necessarily requires. Any conduct of a slave inconsistent with due subordination contravenes the purpose of these acts. . . . The prohibition of whatever is inconsistent with the relation established is of course implied." To this opinion of the majority of the court there was a strong dissenting opinion in which Justice O'Neal! takes the ground that the subordination of the one race to the other is "mere bench legislation," holding that specific enactment was necessary to make an act criminal; he further thought such a theory would lead to harm.

The extreme conservative policy of the law-making body toward any change in the direction of a more liberal policy was felt by public men of the time as is evidenced in the following statement of a case by Judge Withers in 1850 :

"Our fundamental code, now time-honored, is that of 1740. It was enacted soon after a violent, barbarous and somewhat servile bloody attack at Stono. Not a few of its provisions took their hue from the exigency of the occasion, and that it has faded somewhat in the lapse of time is only the usual inevitable consequence of all police systems in the shape of positive terms, which cannot have the quality to keep up with the advancement of a community." This tendency not to interfere in changing the slave code appeared in the failure of the General Assembly to heed the urgent request of Governor Wilson in his annual message in 1824 for a complete revision of these laws. The slave being denied many of the rights granted to free whites, such as self-defense or the pursuit of his own happiness, some apparent compensation was attempted in an analogy, drawn possibly from Roman law or the natural justice of the situation which suggested the family relationship that ought in a measure to exist between the slave and the master. The religious literature, sermons and other documents having to do with the betterment of the condition of the slave almost uniformly held the slaveowner responsible before God for the moral and religious life of his slave, on the ground that he is placed in a sort of patriarchal relationship to his ward, who is not a chattel merely but also a person in the moral sense. Judge O'Neall, who wrote many of the decisions of the highest court on slavery questions and whose book, "The Slave Law of South Carolina," while it may bear the earmarks of haste, is still a most valuable compendium with comment on the legal phases of slavery, appears to have been in the forefront in a progressive interpretation of the slave system in the direction of its amelioration! In the case of Tennent vs. Dendy, decided in 1837, speaking for the Court of Appeals, Judge O'Neall said of slaves if

"They are human beings with passions and feelings like our own and with the same capability of right and wrong action. They, if in a state of nature, would have the right of self-protection which is given by the great Creator to every human being. Their transfer from a state of nature to a state of slavery in society has not destroyed the right of personal protection; it has taken it from the slave and given it to the master.... In the relation of master and servant the dependence of the latter on the former alone for protection cannot be too much encouraged. The slave ought to be fully aware that his master is to him what the best administered government is to the good citizen, a perfect security from injury. When this is the case the relation of master and servant becomes little short of that of parent and child—it commences in the weakness of the one and the strength of the other. Its benefits produce the corresponding consequences of deep and abiding grateful attachments from the slave to the master, and hence result [many] instances of devotion." DeBow in his "Review" bears out this idea in a somewhat practical way by saying that usually slaves were more willing to obey an order if they knew that it came from the master direct than if it was merely from the overseer. This feeling would indicate that a sort of filial reverence for the master was showing itself in a recognition of his paternal relationship to them.

Recognizing this same principle of the family relationship twenty years before the rendering of the above decision the court maintained that a slave owner could be held liable in a civil suit for care and medical attention rendered by a physician who had cared for a slave that had been ill-treated and driven from home by her master. The court cites as a parallel case that of a wife driven from her husband's home by the husband and destitute, arguing that the person who should provide her the necessities of life could recover damages of the husband. The court says:

"The master is bound by the most solemn obligation to protect his slave from suffering, he is bound by the same obligations to defray the expenses or services of another to preserve the slave from pain and danger. The slave lives for his master's service. His time, his labor, his comforts, are all at his master's disposal. The duty of humane treatment and of medical assistance when clearly necessary ought not to be withholden." The act of 1740 protected a slave who committed a crime in defense of his master. This quasi-feudal regulation seems inconsistent with the rule that no slave was allowed to protect himself in self-defense against a white man. The latter was probably made with a view to a more complete subjection of the black to the white race; the former with a view to encourage his making the master's interest his own interest, the purpose being then to hold the master responsible for the consequences. Furthermore a slave committing a crime at the command of the master is not to be held responsible. If "the slave acting without a will but by his master's compulsion" should commit a homicide "he would be the bloody instrument of his cruelty, but might be guilty of no legal offense; the master would be guilty of murder." A slave who had killed another slave in Charleston was acquitted by a court for the trial of slaves in 1847 on the ground that he was acting on the authority of his mistress. The news item shows further that the case against the owner was docketed for the approaching term of court.

There was another legal disability under which the slave labored. He could not bring an action of any kind in court in his own name. He could not prosecute for a battery, nor enter civil suit. He could not even begin legal proceedings to test his right to freedom. Only in the name of another, a white man as "next friend," could a test be made. What is said of the slave in this respect is applicable to the free negro. In the case of the slave, the master was supposed to be the judge of whether an action was necessary; and in the case of the free negro some white person must become sufficiently interested in the cause to act as a "next friend."

Because of the primitive condition of the slaves and free negroes and their lack of moral responsibility they were not admitted as witnesses competent to give evidence against a white person. It appears, however, that no specific law prevented the introduction of negro evidence against a white person, but that his legal disability as a witness was regarded as an axiom of law and common sense. The concessions made him in this respect arise more from the necessity of the circumstances of his relations than by his right.

But from the first a slave's confession before the negro court was admitted as a plea in answer to any charge against him. His testimony, too, was admissible against another slave or free negro against whom no "Christian evidence" is presented and such slave or free negro was, according to the act of 1712, not to be convicted of an offense for which the penalty was loss of "limb or life" except by his own confession or by the "plain and positive evidence of two negroes or slaves, so circumstanced that there shall not be sufficient reason to doubt the truth" of their testimony and after the court has ascertained that they "bear no malice" to the accused. An exception to this was to be made in the case of murder in which the evidence of one slave might be sufficient if to the justice his testimony appeared to be plausible. The act of 1740 following this made it clear that these regulations for the trial of slaves were applicable in toto to free negroes as well as slaves.

There were, however, indirect ways in which a negro's testimony might come to form a part of the evidence before a court of record. Information as to his bodily health confided to a physician, which formed a part of the doctor's physical examination of the slave, would be admissible as evidence. The record of a court for negroes containing the confession of a slave as a part of evidence on which the slave was convicted of a felony might be given in the evidence in the trial of a free white man as an accessory before the fact.

In 2 Brevard Law Cases, page 145, is given a very short report of the case of the State vs. McDowell, heard in 1807, on an appeal from conviction for assault in Greenville district, in which it appears that a free man of color had been admitted as a witness for the prosecution against a white man. It reads in part:

"On motion it was determined in this court by all the judges that any person of color, if the issue of a free white woman, is entitled to give evidence and ought to be admitted as a witness in our courts."

This pronouncement of the court seems to be somewhat out of the ordinary as compared with later decisions. It must have been that the fairness of the hearing in this particular case, owing possibly to some peculiar circumstances, was evident and that the ends of justice had been served. Hence in absence of any statutory provision to the contrary, "on motion" the judges determined what "ought" to be done.

The highest court in two later instances, 1821 and again in 1831, stated, in the first, that a free person of color "is an incompetent witness, in any case, where the rights of white persons are concerned." In the latter it said in part : "A free person of color is not a competent witness, in any case, in the courts of record of this state, although both the parties to the suit are of the same class with himself."

In 1751 an act, after relating that there had been several executions of slaves for poisoning, and after providing for a more vigorous punishment of such offenses, offered to any slave or free negro who would give information of an attempt of any slave to poison his master a reward of four pounds provided such information led to the slave's conviction. But if any slave should suffer as a result of any such testimony which afterwards turned out to be false, the unfaithful witness was subjected to the same penalty as is assessed for the crime. The difficulty here was probably as it was later: it was difficult to get one slave to inform against another. Mr. Seabrook, in a pamphlet on the management of slaves, published in 1834, says that this was one of the things that most interfered with the police control of the slaves. Again, the negro was used to effect in securing evidence against persons charged with negro trading and liquor selling.

While perhaps it is true that the slaves were a closed group on smaller offenses like petty theft, they would betray more serious crimes of their fellows. It was in this way that the proposed Camden insurrection of 1816 was disclosed. In 1817 the General Assembly authorized the Governor to purchase the freedom of the servant, appropriating $1,100 for the purpose and providing an annual pension of $50 for him after he should be set free.   A lasting debt of gratitude was, of course, considered to be due faithful slaves who revealed the plot for an uprising in Charleston in 1822, which the Legislature meeting soon after sought to repay by voting Peter, a slave belonging to John C. Prioleau, the expenses of his emancipation and an annual pension of $50 during his lifetime, or in case he should prefer to remain in servitude or his master should refuse to set him free the annual allowance was to be increased to $100. It may interest the reader to know that this same negro, who it appears did actually secure his freedom, was still living in 1857, and that the Legislature not forgetful of his services, raised his pension to $200 per annum to be paid in quarterly installments.

16

CHAPTER III. The Overseer

An overseer was necessary for the proper control and management of the negroes on a plantation. He was not only an economic necessity to the plantation, but he acquired the character of a plantation quasi-police officer by virtue of the legal provision that all slaveowners were required to have white men on their plantations, in cases where the owners were not resident throughout the year. The Act of 1712 provided a penalty of a fine of forty shillings in the case of any person who should establish and maintain a plantation or stock farm and keep on such farm six "negroes or slaves" without one or more white persons residing on the same. In 1714 the colonial authorities, uneasy on account of the great increase in the number of slaves in the province, laid a duty on the importation of slaves. To this the British slave traders made objection, and the lords proprietors suggested as a substitute that an act be passed requiring every planter to keep at least one white man to every negro on his plantation. Following this there, was an act with the express purpose of encouraging white laborers to settle in the colony which required planters to employ one white man for every ten negroes used, and one white man for every two thousand acres of land held. For every three months the plantation was without this proportion a fine of £10 was to accrue except that one month might be allowed for providing the required number of whites in case any of the whites should run away.

The Act of 1740 recited the following reason for the later provision: "Whereas plantations settled with slaves without any white person thereon may be harbors for runaways and fugitive slaves." It may have been merely to meet the requirements of the letter of the Act of 1712 that a white person lame or decrepit, not capable of managing the negroes on a plantation and not intended to control it was kept on the place where slaves were located. But this act provided that no plantation was to be without a white person for every twenty-five slaves. A fine of twenty shillings for each month during which this regulation was not observed was the penalty. The Act of 1800 required the tax collector to have every slaveholder to take oath that either he lived on his plantation or had a white man for every ten slaves on the plantation. Three months was allowed for the owner to secure another overseer when one left.

Probably with a view to accommodating some slave owners, who on account of malarial conditions did not live on their plantations during the whole of the year, the patrol law of 1819 provided that any slaveowner who did not live on his plantation seven months during the year and who had on it ten working slaves must have an overseer on the place on penalty for failure of a fine of fifty cents per month for each slave. This was interpreted, in 1825, by the Court of Appeals in the case of the State vs. Blythet to mean that a woman who lived on the edge of her plantation for seven months of the year fulfilled the requirements of the law, a woman legally taking the place of a man. The patrol law of 1839 amends the former by substituting a residence of six months for seven and making the maximum number of slaves allowed to live on a plantation without a white man's control fifteen instead of ten. Governor Gist in his annual message in 1859 recommended the revisal of this law so as to require the owner to reside on his plantation during the whole year. The provisions of these last two acts did not and were not intended in any way to supersede the former act of 1740. The latter was to apply more specifically to the small plantations while the earlier law applied to the larger plantations.

This legislation illustrates sectional differences in the state. The climatic conditions in the low lands encouraged the development of large plantations with but few whites on them. Further to the north, where conditions more favorable to the white man prevailed, the two races were more nearly equal in numbers and the smaller farms with few negroes were to be found. In the low country the independent non-slaveholding white farmer had no chance to get a footing on account of the struggle with disease and the competition with slave labor on the large plantation. In the up-country where the farms were smaller in size and greater in number and climatic conditions were more favorable to the white man there was larger opportunity to secure small tracts of land by the non-slaveholding white man. Some of these acquired a few slaves. Accordingly there came to be a class of whites either non-slave holders or small slave owners in the hilly part of the state that formed a distinct class of the people of the community characteristic of the section. In contrast there was almost no such class to be found in the lowlands, where the only social conditions represented were the slaves and their overseers with occasionally an owner living on his own plantation. While the state was a unit in its general slave policy these laws, unnecessary in the northern part of the state, illustrate the different conditions of slavery and the consequent different methods of control or modification of the system where the situation was decidedly different.

Another illustration of differences in legal provisions arising out of differences of conditions in the two sections of the colony was that of an act of 1740 virtually suspending the operation of the patrol service in parts of the state where whites outnumbered the blacks. This exception applied apparently until 1819. It suffices to show the recognition of differences of circumstances and differences of needs in the two sections of the state. Owing to the spread of slavery later it applied to comparatively few districts, but the neglect of patrol duty in some parts of the state may have been due to the same feeling which led to this enactment.

The question arises naturally, how well were these laws enforced? The first observation to be made is that it was decidedly to the interest of the owner both financially and from the point of maintaining order on his plantation to keep such a white person on it. It would be difficult to imagine that the best results could be had from a large plantation entrusted entirely to negroes. And yet Olmsted on one particular farm in South Carolina says that the owner had discussed the unsatisfactory character of most overseers and had said that he depended upon his negro drivers and kept a white overseer merely to carry out the mandates of the law. Perhaps this was an exception to the general rule. It is more likely that some peculiar circumstances prevented compliance in cases where it was not observed than that the main spirit of its provisions was ignored. In 1852 bills of indictment charging two owners with not keeping white men on their plantations were handed to the grand jury of Sumter district but were returned "no bill." There is also the case of the State vs. Blythe, already cited, which appears (by its having been carried to a higher court on appeal) to have gone adversely to the defendant.

The foregoing illustrates how the overseer came to have legal recognition. We now come to some discussion of the overseer as an economic and social factor connected with the institution of slavery. Most of the laws and regulations discussed up to this point were made in behalf of those who might have no interest in a large plantation and yet might suffer depredation from those disorderly slaves as well as in the master's interest, and for the general welfare and peaceable orderliness of society. We now have to look at the overseer as he is related to the master above and the slaves below. So far as he served legitimately the best interests of both he was a factor in society for its well-being. It seems that the overseer was a misfit, a makeshift, and there never grew up a class of men who found this middle position in society satisfactory to themselves or their way of filling it satisfactory to the slaveowners. Indeed, there was nothing in the position to inspire, for even the salary was a bare living. Stern necessity often forbade even a tendency toward kindliness. And on the other side there was much in the calling to destroy the finer sensibilities and make one coarse and brutal. Indeed, one who was too sympathetic or lax was likely to be swamped by the barbarism of the blacks. Those to whom the work most appealed were, perhaps, the least fitted morally and temperamentally for the position. They usually came from among the non-slaveholding, nonpropertied class of whites who at least sometimes may have been distrustful if not jealous of the slaveholder. Overseeing was a step to nothing. The overseer was not often received in the home of the master and certainly not as an equal, and he had few associates that were of an uplifting character. In a sense he, like the slave he controlled, found no hope or ambition in the system.

There was no law or interpretation of the courts to define exactly the overseer's status. He was tacitly regarded as for the time taking the place of the master in his paternal relation of duty and responsibility to the slave. He controlled the movements of the slave, furnishing him the necessary pass when he was to leave the plantation. He had all the rights to chastise the slaves under his care that the master had except as limited by the master. He provided for the slaves, their food allowances and clothes and everything of that kind, as the master would do or as the master from time to time directed. The property interest of the master in his slave was regarded as sufficient to protect the slave from cruelty at the hands of the overseer and was a better guarantee than were the laws against the cruelty of the master toward his own slave. Most masters had some rules more or less elaborate for this purpose. The following extract from one of these contracts between slaveowner and overseer preserved in the collections of the South Carolina Historical Society will illustrate this custom:

"6th. John Ball will ever reserve to himself the right to discharge and turn off John Penny at any time of the year if he gets drunk, or improperly abuses his trust ... or maltreat the negroes under his care .... And if that should unfortunately be the case .... John Ball will pay for the time actually served." But it is here probably that notwithstanding the vigilance of the slaveowner, there crept in on the large plantation much of the cruelty for which the system of slavery has aroused so much criticism. Not that all overseers were evil-minded but that there often did arise provocation to undeserved punishment. And sometimes the revenge of the slaves was wreaked upon the overseer. The Independent Press, of Abbeville, on Aug 5, 1854, notes the murder of an overseer by three negroes in Abbeville district, and on June 17, 1854, the murder of an overseer in Newberry district by a slave.

But we shall allow selections from periodicals of the time and other sources to speak for themselves. The following advertisement appended to another notice in the South Carolina Gazette, of November 7, 1741, suggests that there were some who took advantage of their position as overseer for evil:

"A good overseer is wanted and shall have good encouragement, in case he understands plantation affairs and can behave himself well and be honest." The following "Wanted" gives us a pretty clear idea of the qualifications that the owner desired the overseer to have:

City Gazette and Daily Advertiser, Dec. 1, 1800.

"The subscriber would give good encouragement to a man of the following description: a good cotton and rice planter, sober, honest, industrious, attentive and constantly on the plantation; who understands the management of negroes, to be worked with attention, steadiness and at the same time to be treated with humanity and care.

No other person to be employed and therefore any other application will be needless."

A contributor to the Carolina Planter of February 19, 1840, sets this down as some of the questions an overseer ought to have asked him:

"Whether he is an attentive, careful and humane man? Will he treat negroes well? Keep up their spirit? Attend to the sick; favor the weakly? Take care of the women and children?"

An ex-overseer gives to men of his former calling the following advice as to discipline, which gives us a good picture of control on the plantation:

"It is indispensable that you exercise judgment and consideration in the management of the negroes under your charge. Be firm and at the same time gentle in your control. Never display yourself before them in a passion; and even in inflicting the severest punishment, do so in a mild, cool manner, and it will produce a ten-fold effect. When you find it necessary to use the whip (and as desirable as it would be to dispense with it entirely it is necessary at times) apply it slowly and deliberately to the extent that you are determined in your own mind to be needful before you begin. The indiscriminate, constant and excessive use of the whip is altogether unnecessary and inexcusable. When it can be done without a too great loss of time the stocks offer a means of punishment greatly to be preferred. Never threaten a negro, but if you have occasion to punish do it at once, or say nothing until ready to do so. A passionate and violent threat will often scare the best disposed negro to the woods. Always keep your word with them in punishments as well as rewards. Never forgive that in one which you would punish in another, but treat all alike, showing no favoritism. Never be induced by a course of good behavior by the negroes to relax the strictness of your discipline; but when you have, by judicious management, brought them to that state keep them there by that means. The only way to keep a negro honest is not to trust him. This seems a harsh assertion but it is unfortunately true." Another by "Decater," who from his manner of talk is also an ex-overseer, in the course of a lengthy article in the same periodical of January, 1855, drops this significant remark as to plantation control:

"Let them know that you have a good feeling towards them and they are sure to respect you and obey you and do it willingly. I have found it difficult to do business successfully with them when I have to force everything out of them by the lash." The following very significant characterization of the situation was made by W. B. Seabrook in an address before the United Agricultural Society of South Carolina in 1827: "In general the planter entrusts the sole management of his domestic concerns to some needy wanderer who, without education, without morals or the incentive of honorable emulation, assumes the mastership of a business at once complicated in its details and requiring the unwearied exercise of a sound discretion to conduct it safely through the ordeal of its own peculiar composition. Oftentimes twenty or thirty competent overseers exercise an unlimited control over a whole district [now called county] comprising thousands of laborers. In their hands is truly for a time, the whole fortune of their employers. Their ignorance cannot advance it; their indiscretion may forever blast it and peradventure shake the state to its center. . . . [Footnote made on revisal of address for publication is as follows:] To the gloomy description here given of our overseers there are many and honorable exceptions; and I state with pride and pleasure, that as a class they are gradually improving in morals, education and general worth." A Carolina planter is quoted by Olmsted to the effect that it was more common for an overseer to indulge the slaves in their idleness in order to win their favor and thus prevent their disclosing his faults than it was to whip them too severely. Similarly is Mr. Louis Manigaull's experience as quoted from his plantation record by Professor Phillips as a special instance of an overseer who had broken "long established discipline" by undignified familiarity with the slaves.

On the other hand a contributor to The Carolina Planter of February 19, 1840, already referred to, finds other difficulties. His idea is that the overseer often drives the slaves too hard in order to make a good showing; or again the scarcity of even "tolerable overseers" makes it impossible to lay down strict rules for the welfare of the slaves. There seems to have been a common complaint as to the poor character of the men who were overseers by "undue prejudice indulged against this people" and the poor salaries. "A City Rustic," in the Charleston Mercury of October 6, 1829, indicates that oversight of too many negroes for one leads to inefficiency, carelessness and downright dishonesty of the overseer and that there resulted possibly a twenty-five per cent, leakage of the gross proceeds.

On the plantation there was another manager of quasi-official character who had to do with its management and particularly with the control of its negroes. This was the negro driver chosen from among the slaves themselves. He was a sort of intermediary between the laboring slave and the overseer or his master. He was trusted in varying degrees. Often he carried the keys and was looked upon as a necessary though undesirable adjunct of the plantation. His duties are so well described in the rules laid down by P. C. Weston for the management of his rice plantation that we shall quote:

"Drivers are under the overseer to maintain discipline and order on the place. They are to be responsible for the quiet of the negro houses, for the proper performance of tasks, for bringing out the people early in the morning, and generally for the immediate inspection of such things as the overseer generally superintends." [It is also added that he sees that tasks are satisfactorily completed.] The negro driver was looked upon as a mild innovation by those who did not have such an organization. And it is unquestioned that the opportunities and liberties which he had sometimes abused. In a news note in the Abbeville Banner of February 18, 1848, is mentioned the murder of two negroes by drivers. It is not to be imagined that the driver often abused his privileges, for it was by faithful services that he rose to his superior position. He might have been very much disliked by the other slaves, and might have given good reason for such an unfavorable impression upon them. But would the slaveowners have long tolerated a system which was wholly bad? We shall here quote from an article by a "City Rustic" in the Charleston Mercury of October 2, 1829, for what it is worth as evidence, though the picture is certainly much overdrawn:

"From these causes [i.e., poor supply of good overseers] and from the consequent and unavoidable system of management necessarily and long adopted throughout the lower country, the small planters and their property have fallen into the hands of black drivers, a set of men which there does not exist on the face of the earth any on whom there can be placed less dependence. Practiced in every species of deception from their infancy; leagued together far and nearby common interest, and having all the more intelligent and finished thieves in the neighborhood under their arbitrary control, it is not strange that every avenue to information should be closely shut between the sometimes oppressed slave or the still rarer honest one, and the suffering and deluded master; and that a state productive of the complete demoralization of negroes, with all of its destructive consequences, should be the inevitable result."

26

CHAPTER IV. The Patrol System

Almost from the very first the slave population presented the problem of a police control that would suit the needs of the community and hold in check this irresponsible and often dangerous part of Southern society. For the more serious crimes methods of trial and punishment were provided. But for the general good-ordering and home-keeping of the slave some more exacting method must be employed than mere punishment by a court which the negro very little understood. If the slave had been unhampered in his general movements he would have been rendered capable of insurrection, the greatest possible danger to be feared from the African population. To this one must add the smaller fights, broils and disorders they would probably have had with each other if allowed to go from plantation to plantation without restraint. Finally the master would find the slave much less efficient if allowed the loss of sleep and energy incident to such carousing.

But while this aimless wandering about of the slave was unauthorized there were various errands both by day and by night desired by the master. Again it often occurred that the slave living on one plantation had as his accepted wife a negro woman living on another plantation. This marriage relationship was recognized both by the master and the negro man on the one side and the master and the negro woman on the other. Wednesday and Saturday nights he was usually allowed to be away from his cabin on a visit to his wife. It was evident that there must be some regulation to permit and authorize this if there was to be a general prohibition of wandering. The rule was that no slave should be found off his master's plantation, particularly at night, without a written pass from his master, or in company with some white person, even a child ten years of age, who could vouch for the cause of his absence. The substance of the pass was an order to any person or patrolman to permit the slave "to pass and repass" from a given hour on a certain day to a given hour on some following day. The law of 1734 made it necessary that the pass show the destination of the slave and if he rides a horse it was to be so stated. It appears, however, that the pass usually gave permission merely to the slave to be absent from the plantation for a given length of time. And even if such permit was not all that was understood to be legally required, it was generally accepted as sufficient by the patrol. Later the Constitutional Court decided that a pass did not have to indicate the destination of the slave. But the law was that a general pass intended to be good over a long period of time to permit the free coming and going of the slave would not be recognized by the patrol, nor were they authorized to accept such a pass, as its purpose was to evade the spirit of the patrol police laws by the master. The frequency of complaints like the following suggests that the law was not observed. In a communication appearing in The Daily Telegraph of Nov. 4, 1848, as to the policing of the negroes occurs this statement as to passes:

"A 'general pass' (as it is called) to enable a slave to go at large, when and where he pleases, is an outrage on the community, illegal in itself and will no longer be recognized. With a proper and specific pass a slave is always safe." Concerning which the editor remarks:

"We hardly deem it necessary to say one word on the subject of passes or permits; it must be obvious to everyone, that where they neither limit the bearer to time or place, gross abuses must necessarily arise under them; and we presume all such passes are illegal, and therefore will be disregarded." The free movement of the slaves concerned not only the immediate owner but every other individual in the community as well, for it afforded opportunity to the slave to instigate and co-operate in insurrectionary schemes; also it afforded opportunity for stealing, the colored person's inherent weakness. Often these passes were given by members of the master's family with, of course, the master's tacit consent, the latter's name appearing on the permit. Any person who forged a pass was to be severely punished, the maximum penalty being $1,000 fine and twelve months imprisonment. The sessions journal of Marlborough district in 1853 records the trial and acquittal of a white man for giving a ticket to the slave of another. He had been held for trial under a bond for $1,000. It is probable that there was a suspicion of his aiding in the escape of the slave as this was a common way of getting the slave out of the community. Another similar case occurred in Greenville 1847 but neither appears to have come to trial. The written pass was not required by day in the incorporated towns. The slaves were allowed to go about from place to place in town in the day time on errands of the master, most of the slaves being known to the local police force. But at night after nine o'clock it was necessary for them to have a permit from the master.

The evolution of the patrol system is interesting. The need of keeping the slaves from roving was felt from the very first. Among the earliest of the colonial acts in 1686 is one that gave any person the right to apprehend, properly chastise, and send home any slave who might be found off his master's plantation without a ticket. This plan was not altogether effective, and in 1690 it was made the duty of all persons under penalty of forty shillings to arrest and chastise any slave out of his home plantation without a proper ticket. This plan of making it everybody's business to punish wandering slaves seems to have been sufficient at least for a time.

In 1704 the governor and council passed a law that in time of public danger when the forces of the colony were likely to be drawn toward the coast for defense the general of all the forces should appoint from each company of militia one or more captains who, on the nomination of the general, shall each select ten men "to ride" the districts, taking up any strolling negroes that might be found off their master's plantation without a ticket. It would appear then that the interest in the common good made the patrol provisions of the act of 1690 as yet all that was needed; or we are to guess that the negroes were more or less orderly, and that it was in time of "alarm" that they were disorderly or then that the danger from insurrection was greatest. The preamble of the act of 1704 stated its purposes to be "to prevent such insurrections and mischiefs as from the great number of slaves we have reason to suspect may happen when the greater part of the inhabitants are drawn together." This probably accounts for the old name sometimes applied to the patrolmen, "alarm men."

This also explains how the police patrol came to be a part of the military. The act of 1721 merged the patrol service definitely into the militia organization, making it a part of the military system, and devolving upon the military authority its arrangement and maintenance. This feature was continued until 1860. The reason for the arrangement is cited in the preamble of the act:

"Whereas the several patrols in this province generally consist of the choicest and best men, who screen themselves from doing such services in alarms as are required and ought to be done by men of their ability which creates great murmurings and disturbances in the militia in this Province." Apparently efforts to evade patrol service were common. Indeed, it was a thankless task throughout the reign of the landlord slaveholder.

In 1734 a regular patrol, by act of the Provincial Assembly, was organized, reciting in its preamble the reasons and needs therefor as follows:

"Whereas former acts of the assembly passed in the province for regulating patrols have not answered the intention thereof and it being highly necessary to the well-being of the province that the several patrols should be rendered as useful as possible in the keeping all slaves in due order."

The provisions of this act form the basis of all later patrol legislation. Later acts modified and elaborated this primitive law, but the main principles of the patrol system as herein expressed for the next century and a quarter remained the same. The "beat company"—by which is meant the group of five men who rode over the plantations and looked after the correction of disorders—was to be composed of a captain and four other men of the regular militia appointed from time to time. The patrolmen were to receive compensation, the captain £50 per annum and each of the others £25, and exemption from all other military service. For each district there were to be appointed three commissioners as supervisors of the patrol. The duties of this patrol were to visit each plantation in its beat at least once per month, chastising any slave found absenting himself from home without a pass, administering twenty lashes as a maximum; to search the negro dwellings, confiscating any firearms that might be in the home or any goods that they might have good reason to believe have been stolen; to enter any tippling house or any other house whatever, where any one of them might have seen a slave enter. Any fowls or provisions found in the hands of any negro who is away from home without a ticket might be appropriated to the patrolman's own use. The provincial acts usually expired after three years. Hence this law was re-enacted in 1737 with some changes. By the later act ministers were exempt from serving on the patrol; the patrolmen chose their own captain; visits on duty were to be once every week so as to reach every plantation at least once each month; confiscated goods were to be delivered to the commissioners of the patrol. It was also provided that in case any information in a cabal or any kind of unlawful meeting of negroes should come to the ears of any officer of the patrol or militia he might summon, on penalty for failure, a number of persons necessary for dispersing the same. A more significant change, however, was one limiting the choice of patrolmen to fifty-acre freeholders or forty-shilling tax payers; to this was attached the following proviso: "provided always that the said commissioners shall not enlist any person as a voluntary patrolman." We are left here to conjecture whether irresponsible persons had been attracted by the pay which must have been considerable for that time and hence had caused dissatisfaction on the part of the owners; or that others who had no intimate interest in the slave property of the community joined in voluntarily as on a holiday excursion or for the purpose of wreaking vengeance for an imaginary or real grievance.

The patrol act of 1740 stated, in section 10—

"Many irregularities have been committed by former patrols arising chiefly from their drinking too much liquor before or during the time of their riding on duty." From this it would appear that even at best there was often considerable disorderly conduct among the patrolmen, and some of the "irregularities" may have been unauthorized whipping of slaves who were duly provided with passes, or undue disturbance of slaves who were peaceably at home. These were grievances that slaveowners of a later day resented. At this time there may have been considerable distrust of the non-slaveholder by the slaveholder, or, this exclusion of the non-slaveholder may have been to relieve him of services in a cause for which he was not responsible.

When the time for re-enacting the patrol law came again in 1740, just following the Stono insurrection, a general tightening up of the slave regulations was indulged in as well as a general revision of the negro law. By the provisions of this law the captain of the militia company was to keep a list of all persons liable for patrol duty, though not owning or being interested in a slave sixteen years old to be excepted, while female slaveowners were required to furnish a substitute. The ridings in each beat were not to include any circuit of more than fifteen miles. The captain was required at each muster to "prick off" a certain number, not more than seven, located near together, to do patrol duty until the next muster. If any person should fail to respond for duty, the captain was authorized to employ a substitute at thirty shillings per night to be collected from the defaulter by action for debt. A substitute of an age between sixteen and sixty years could be sent by a regular patrolman. This act was not to apply where the whites were in numbers superior to the blacks. Mention was here made of the switch or cowhide as the instrument with which the castigation was to be administered.

The patrol laws seem to have remained practically untouched from 1740 to 1819. Perhaps the difficulty, if any, lay in their administration. For example the Charleston grand jury in 1766 said:

"We present as a general grievance through the province the want of patrol duty being duly done, and submit to the legislature whether a provincial or parochial tax to support the expense of a standing patrol to be on constant duty would not better answer the purpose of apprehending slaves." In 1772 the grand jury at the court held in Camden said: "We present as a Grievance the Patrol Act not being put in Force, whereby many Villanies and Robberies are committed which otherwise in a great measure might be prevented." Governor Drayton in his annual message in 1800 suggested the patrol laws as a proper subject for revision. Governor Hamilton in his annual message in 1805, speaking of the patrol laws, said:

"It is a fact that in the lower parts of the state, where regulations of this kind are particularly needed, those who are most interested in the preservation of peace and order, have, from a mistaken notion of things, thrown the whole of this burden on others less fortunately circumstanced, on whom alone the present penalty is coercive. Permit me, therefore, to recommend the imposition of a fine for default, in proportion of the property of the individual, to be rated by his tax return, as in the case for non-performance of militia duty." Again the next year he somewhat elaborated the same idea, prefacing his remark with a statement possibly exaggerated, it is true, since the legislature seems to have thought the patrol laws quite sufficient for the next thirteen years. He said:

"The last of which [the patrol laws] is so deficient as to coercive principle, that it has become a thing merely without effect." In 1816 Governor Williams was led by two attempted insurrections in the year just passed to seek a remedy in some amendment of the laws and a general tightening up of the regulations. He says:

"These incidents [the Camden and Ashepoo attempts at insurrection] admonish us to a careful revisal of our patrol system. Perhaps the agents selected for its execution are proper; but the responsibility under which they act is believed to be inadequate to a just administration of it. If the duties to be performed by the agents are to be considered of a military nature wholly, as by some they have been, no evil could result from having superior officers to superintend their execution; if of a civil character, the aid of the court of law might be successfully resorted to, by adding an additional clause in the oath administered to the grand jurors." But for a general revision of the patrol laws the General Assembly waited until 1819. By the act of the legislature of that year all white males over eighteen were made liable for patrol duty, the non-slaveholders being excused from service after reaching the age of forty-five. Substitutes from eighteen to sixty years old could be sent by persons liable for service. Governor Hamilton's suggestion, made thirteen years before, was embodied in the act by fixing the penalty for non-performance of patrol duty at a fine of $2.00 plus ten per cent of the delinquent's last tax levy. This was sufficient to reach the person whose wealth made a mere fine of $2.00 light. A patrolman finding arms in a slave's house was allowed to appropriate them to his own use by making oath before a magistrate as to the manner of their seizure after the owner of the slave had had an opportunity to be heard. To preserve the orderliness of the patrol while on duty a fine of $5.00 was to be imposed by his military superior upon a captain of patrol for misbehavior and a fine of $2.00 upon a private patrolman for disorderliness or disobedience to the orders of the captain. The act also provided for imposing a fine of $5.00 upon a person for beating a negro unlawfully, that is one who was either quietly at home or was travelling with a ticket. These provisions as to the patrol were made not to apply within an incorporated town. To make the operations of the patrol as unhampered as possible it was enacted that any person prosecuting the patrols for any act of theirs in the performance of their duty, in case the prosecutor should lose his case, should forfeit a sum three times the costs. The captain of each beat company was to make a return at stated times to his superior officers of the militia as to how the duties of the patrolmen entrusted to him had been performed on penalty of a fine of $20 for failure. In at least one case such a penalty was enforced by a court martial which was declared by the Court of Appeals in 1840 to be the proper kind of procedure.

Another apparently unfortunate provision permitted any person to act in the capacity of a patrolman in administering punishment if at any time he should find a slave out of his home place. This probably led to abuses and was finally abolished in 1839. Beating a slave who was found away from his master's premises but who had a ticket was to be construed legally as abusing a slave.

To summarize a few phases of the development of the patrol system will serve to unify what has been given somewhat in detail. To correct the strolling slave, allowed as a privilege to the white man at first, was soon afterwards made his duty. As a precaution against disturbances from the negroes in times of public danger when the number of the white settlers was small a detachment of the militia was authorized "to ride" the districts. The same kind of policing in times of peace was found to be necessary as early as 1734. The practicability of the use of civilians for this purpose under a military organization known as the "beat company" was soon demonstrated. Limitations of the service to freeholders with compensation were removed in 1819 and all white males were made liable for duty without compensation. Apparently evasion of duty was common; disorderliness of the patrol was unfortunately frequent; at times interference with the patrol in the performance of their duties occurred. All of these weaknesses the act of 1819 sought to overcome and in large measure by this act the system was perfected.

The proper enforcement of the patrol laws was at all times the difficult feature of the police control of the slaves. In 1820, the year following the enactment of the elaborate patrol law of 1819, Governor Geddes in his annual message says:

"The patrol duty which is so intimately connected with the good order and police of the state, is still so greatly neglected in several of our parishes and districts, that serious inconveniences have been felt and cannot fail to continue, unless additional amendments are made to the law on this subject, as the performance of the duty it imposes cannot be enforced." No new law followed as the result of this recommendation, the Legislature probably realizing that there was but little that additional enactment could accomplish. Time alone could accustom men to the more formally imposed duties. In the spring of 1823 an indictment was brought in Union district for "Neglect of duty as Capt. of Patrols" and the defendant was convicted in the fall of the next year, the sentence being a fine of $20 and the costs of the prosecution; the record shows that the fine was paid. It is significant that this is the only incident of a conviction for non-performance of patrol duty that the available criminal records of the nine counties visited by the writer revealed. As late as 1853 the following appears in the presentment of the Williamsburg grand jury:

"We present as a grievance the general neglect of the Provisions of the Patrole Law." And in pursuance of this the presiding judge makes the following order:

"So much of said presentment as complains of the general neglect of the Patrol law be served on, Colonel of this regiment, and he be requested to extend the same to the captains of the various Beat Companies throughout the District." As a general statement the patrol laws were probably well enforced somewhat effectively in the rural districts. This does not mean necessarily that the ridings were always regularly distributed but they were usually so. It appears that these ridings were more or less regular in the country districts. Any disturbance or great prevalence of thieving by the negroes was likely to be sufficient to bring pressure to bear upon the patrol to ride their beats regularly. But when all was quiet and orderly and there was apparently no danger of any kind it is not at all improbable that the patrol was lulled into inactivity and many of the ridings were neglected. The fact that the master usually disliked for his slave to fall into the hands of the patrol because he was often "beaten up" is sufficient evidence that the non-slaveholder looked upon the patrol as the guarantee of his safety from evils often perpetrated by the black race.

The case of the State vs. Cole, Dauner and Gaskins heard in 1822, gives a picture of the seamy side of the enforcement of the system. A slaveowner was aroused in the dead of the night by an unseemly noise, occasioned by the presence of the patrol, and going out he found his dog had been killed, a slave peaceably at home had been severely whipped, and on his appearance he himself was abused in harsh language. The testimony showed that this occurred several times. Another similar case arose in 1824. A young man who claimed to be acting under the orders of his father, who was captain of the patrol, entered the house of a white man during the owner's absence and took away a gun while the house was in the possession of a slave. In both cases the highest court held that the acts were unlawful and that damages could be maintained. It appears, however, that in order to uphold the patrol system and to allow patrolmen to feel that they were to have a reasonably free hand, many unlawful things were indulged in and either went unpunished or were punished with only insignificant fines. This, it seems, was the greatest evil of the system for it gave unscrupulous persons unfair advantages and appears not to have encouraged the enforcement of the law by the better class. It was possibly in protest against what he regarded as unwarranted and unlawful interference of the patrol that a white person was found guilty in the sessions court of Marlborough district in 1846 for "resisting patrol" and sentenced to two weeks imprisonment and a fine of $2.00.

The following quotation from a case occurring in Newberry district, to which reference will again be made, shows the very large discretionary latitude allowed to the patrol even to the extent of ignoring legal provisions to carry out the spirit of the law:

"Let the patrol always act in the spirit that should guide the discreet, sedate, intelligent and humane owner of slaves and they will find the judicial arm of the government nerved to sustain them, indeed if it could be presumed that in such case they would ever need it. Thus guided they may often find occasion—no doubt they will—to overlook a harmless violation, a venial transgression of the strict letter." The court then made this general observation:

"An attentive examination, however, of our slave law will show that there are few occasions when a slave is supposed to need the interposition of police discipline, whether wielded by the public or private arm, when his errand from home is known to his owner and permitted him in writing." The other side of unlawful interference had been clearly reproved in 1819 by the same court:

"It is highly proper to protect these officers [patrols] when acting within the limits of their authority; but nothing is so offensive to the law, as to violate the principles of justice and humanity under the semblance of its authority.... It would be a violation of all law to place the slaves of the country at the mercy of every unprincipled and unfeeling man who may be clothed with this brief authority. It is the duty as well as the interest of every master to protect his slave from unnecessary punishment and to resist the abuse of legal authority." In Union district in 1818 and again in 1821 and in Spartanburg in 1832 bills of indictment for "assaulting patrole" and for "opposing patrole" were put in the hands of the grand jury by the solicitor, but in none of the three cases was a true bill returned. In the Spartanburg case the papers including sworn evidence are accessible. They show that a white man interfered with the patrol which was whipping certain negroes who were away from home without passes at two o'clock at night. Whether the negroes were at the white man's house or at the cabins of his own slaves does not appear; but the available facts suggest the probability that they were loafing in or about the white man's own home and that the patrol suspected some evil like gaming to be their purpose. The fact that the white man interfered points to his having had some interest in their presence.

As before mentioned, the act of 1819 had modified the general provisions on patrol regulations by making it unlawful to chastise slaves in any incorporated town who were found on the streets without a ticket from daylight until 9 p.m., provided their home was with their master whose residence was in the city. This law of 1819 was a rural police act. The effort to apply the same police regulations even to the smaller towns that were applicable to the plantation was to hamper the legitimate industrial operations in the town. It was found necessary to turn over the patrol duties to the regular police force. But these changes were gradual. Probably owing to the scare of the attempted insurrection near Camden in 1816, that town by a special act of 1818 had had transferred to its town council the entire control and management of the patrol and the enforcing of the patrol regulations.

This act provided that "the members of the town council . . . . shall be subject to the same penalties for neglect of patrol duty that the captains of beat companies are now subject to by law." Probably some difficulty in enforcing the patrol law arose for in 1830 another act was passed allowing the town council the right to enforce duty by a fine of $20 and to provide for the commutation of service by a payment in lieu of services.

Columbia was given, by an act of 1823, the right to regulate through its intendant and wardens the operation and manner of enforcing the patrol system. The supply bill ordinance of the city in 1852 provided for a commutation tax of $3.00 instead of serving as a patrol. A similar commutation tax of $4.00 per annum in lieu of patrol service was provided by an ordinance for Camden in 1841.

It seems that village patrol service was well enforced—Charleston excepted—by the marshal of the town. It had the effect probably of driving from the town to points outside the corporate limits the evil doers among the slaves and free negroes as will appear from the following quotations occurring in a communication to The Daily Telegraph (Columbia), of Nov. 4, 1848, from "A Citizen of the Sandhills."

"The latter [i. e., people living just outside the town] have long been subjected to aggressions and annoyances of various kinds from these negroes, who from notoriously bad character, are forced by dread of the marshal to betake themselves beyond the limits of the town in pursuit of their evil practices which evil has suddenly been much increased by the influx of laborers on the railroads going forward.

"Unusual vigilance is now required and henceforward patrol law will be rigidly enforced in the different beats. The residents of the sand hills are determined to abate the nuisance in the most summary and effectual manner practicable.

"It is time to put a stop to this marauding when burglary has commenced, after the smoke-houses and poultry yards are exhausted—and when a nest of gamblers can be fallen upon almost every night in the week—every Sunday certainly.

"To flee from the patrol when challenged—to resist, effect or attempt an escape, when arrested, has become so common with the scoundrels of late, that a few startling examples must be made." Not all the regulations, particularly the patrol regulations dealing with slaves, applied to free negroes, who were allowed freedom of movement from place to place without legal restraint. Where their numbers were considerable they, however, presented much the same problem of control that the slaves did. Hence curfew laws applicable to free negroes as well as slaves were resorted to. As early as 1804 Charleston passed such an ordinance.

Charleston Courier, Dec. 3, 1804.

The town of Pendleton, in the foothills, which, according to the census of 1830, had only 329 inhabitants—172 whites and 157 slaves—had a curfew ordinance in force in 1835, providing that the patrol should "apprehend and correct all slaves and free persons of color" who might be found on the streets after 9 p. m. "whether such slave or free person of color have a pass or not." Probably other if not all towns and villages had such regulations for clearing the streets at night.

The proper policing of the colored population seems to have been a greater problem in Charleston than elsewhere, due in large part no doubt to the lax rein held over them and to the presence there of a larger number of free negroes than elsewhere. The regulations had to be more flexible, for owners often hired out their slaves whose coming and going when in the legitimate performance of their duties were less circumscribed than they were on the plantations. At every angle of the negro's activity there was more opportunity of taking advantage of his liberties for evil. And yet many of the evils were often probably not worse than aimless loitering or congregating on the streets on public occasions.

These grievances as to the control of the negro population go back to the early times. It seems that the port of Charleston very soon became a sort of rendezvous for these undesirables. The seventh section of the Negro law of 1712 says that,

"Whereas great numbers of slaves which do not dwell in Charleston on Sundays and holidays resort hither to drink, fight, curse and swear and profane the Sabbath and using and carrying of clubs and other mischievous weapons, resorting in great companies together, which may give them an opportunity for executing any wicked designs and purposes to the damage and prejudice of the inhabitants of this province." The section after thus reciting the evils makes it the duty of the constable of Charleston on Sundays, Christmas, Whitsuntide and

Easter to press into service as many men as might be necessary to go through all the streets and to search the houses and publicly to whip all slaves found visiting and then turn them over to the marshal to be dealt with as runaways. The patrol law of 1734, before referred to, provided in a special section for two patrols of eight men each to make alternate ridings, on Saturday nights, Sundays, Sunday nights and holidays.

These laws did not have all of the effect desired. The Charleston grand jury in 1744 said:

"We present as a grievance the great insolence of negroes in Charles Town by gaming in the streets and caballing in great numbers through most parts of the Town, especially on the Sabbath day."

Another presentment of similar import was made by the grand jury in 1766:

"We present that the negro law is not put into strict execution, and that the slaves of Charleston are not under a good regulation, and that they at all times in the night go about the streets rioting, that they do often gather in great numbers on the Sabbath day and make riots where it is not in the power of the small number of watchmen to suppress them, which may without any precaution prove the utmost ill consequences to this province."

That the enforcement of the patrol was either necessarily or carelessly lax appears in the following presentment of the grand jury in the next year:

"We present as a grievance the bad practice of free negroes and mulattoes being suffered to pass to and fro without any certificate or badge of their being free, by which means many runaway slaves are suffered to pass as free."

The need of something like a guard-house with the correction idea for these colored offenders against police regulations became evident and took form in the workhouse scheme. It appears at first to have been intended for other servants as well as slaves but soon came to be used solely for negroes. It must have been regarded as a thankless task, since the first section of the ordinance providing for its management by the commissioners attaches a penalty of a fine of $40 for refusal by any person to serve in that capacity when he had been chosen by the city council. Still there seems to have been but little reason for such an idea, if it did exist, for the workhouse appears to have been an instance of an intelligent method of dealing with the troublesome problem of police control. It may be disagreeable to administer the affairs of a prison and inflict the punishment provided for, but so long as we have criminals, they must be dealt with in some way by somebody in the interest of society.

This is the way an Englishman travelling in America in 1827 regarded the purpose of the workhouse:

"It seems, indeed an essential part of the system of slavery that the lash should be used as a means of enforcing discipline. But as the disagreeable nature of this discipline prevents the master from administering it at home, the offending slave is sent to the workhouse with a note and piece of money, on delivering which he receives so many stripes and is sent back again." To this workhouse were sent slaves and free negroes arrested by the police or patrol after beating of tattoo, or arrested runaways. "Lodged in the workhouse at the pleasure of the owner" (who became liable for the costs of the slave's arrest and detention) was the usual form. Any slaveowner had the privilege of placing an unruly or disobedient slave in the workhouse for correction for any length of time and by paying for his dieting the slave might be allowed to remain for some time without work. For each correction, whipping or putting on of irons a fee of twenty-five cents was charged. The master of the workhouse was limited by ordinance to administer not more than two whippings of twenty lashes each in any one week and at least three days must intervene, even though the owner might desire more severe and more frequent castigation. This made it unnecessary for the owner to whip his own slave if he found it distasteful, and perhaps the threat of a trip to the workhouse had a salutary effect on the slave's conduct. It is not at all likely that it made the corporal punishment of the slave more cruel, for the master of the workhouse was limited in this respect and chastisement was at the owner's direction and avoided the cruelty incident to sudden heat of passion. It also provided a convenient place of commitment. All the inmates of the workhouse were employed in gainful occupations— stone cutting was one—during their stay unless unable or their master requested remission of labor.

In 1804 the Charleston city council passed a curfew law, which provided that any free negro being found without his own or his employer's premises after beating of tattoo should be lodged in the guard-house until a fine ranging from $1 to $5 be paid by himself or in the case of a slave by his owner. If the money should not be forthcoming he was to work it out at the workhouse. Refusal to stand when arrested or to be obstinate at trial was to be punished with a fine of $40. But this regulation was not unattended with difficulty. In a communication from "Investigator," in The Southern Patriot of December 22, 1823, complaint was made that often when a slave is arrested another negro, presumably free, was allowed by the warden of the guard-house to pay the fine and secure the slave's release. It was not claimed that this occurred frequently and perhaps was rare. "Investigator" raised the inquiry to know whether this practice had the approval of the city council or whether it was a usurpation by the wardens of the guard-house. For he added that it might be that the master by this means did not learn of the absence of his slave from his quarters and would wish to have him punished if he did know it.

There were several other minor ordinances which in all probability were not well enforced. An ordinance of 1813 prohibited negroes from swearing, smoking or walking with a cane on the streets—the infirm or blind were allowed use of a cane of course—or to making any joyful demonstration. No negro dances were to be held without the consent of the city wardens, nor were negroes to assemble at any military parade. This last was not well enforced as appears from the following from "Enquirer," on "Our Police," in the Charleston Mercury of December 10, 1835:

"At all our military parades our streets are crowded and infested with troops of negroes, who neglect their master's work to attend these parades. Why is the law not enforced?" Another regulation in 1848 excluded from the parks all slaves and free negroes unless in company with a white person, or unless they had passes from their masters, or in case of free negroes, from their employers, and these passes must be for a specific purpose. This was appropriate if they congregated on the batteries and wharves. "A Friend of Good Order" complained, in the Charleston Courier of December 11, 1821, that the street on South Bay was taken up with riotous negroes. Another ordinance of 1850 prohibited, with a penalty for its violation by a fine of $5 to $20, any owner of a saloon to allow a slave or free negro to loiter or sit down in his place of business. The report of Wm. Porcher Miles, referred to again, points out that whiskey is the greatest evil to combat in policing the negroes of the city. A summing up of the cases against negroes in the police court as they were written up for the Evening News in 1856 shows that drunkenness was a part of the charge in almost all of the cases.

The following excellent summary of the negro cases by Mayor Robert Y. Hayne, for the year ending September 1, 1837, as given in his annual report, affords us a clear statement of the dealings of his court with the colored population for a year favorable for a fair comparison of results:

"The number of slaves [i. e., brought before the mayor's court] was 768, of whom 138 were discharged, 309 fined, 264 committed to the work-house, or subjected for trial.

"The number of free persons of color was 78, of whom 27 were discharged, 36 fined or subjected to corporal punishment, 5 committed to the workhouse, and 10 committed for trial

"Of the 573 slaves fined or committed to the workhouse nearly the whole were arrested for being out at night without tickets or being found in the dram shops or other unlawful places. The fines imposed did not in general exceed $1, and where corporal punishment was inflicted it was always moderate. It is worthy to remark that of the 460 cases reported by the marshals for prosecution, but 22 were actually prosecuted, the penalties having been voluntarily paid in 303 cases, and in 118 cases having been remitted, thus preventing by a previous examination, 421 suits." From the report two years later of the proceedings of the city authorities is taken the following extract relating to the colored population:

"The following is a statement of the number of cases examined, and of the manner in which they were disposed of, in which slaves and free persons of color were arrested for being "out after the beating of the tattoo without tickets, fighting and rioting in the streets, following military companies, walking on the battery contrary to law, bathing horses at forbidden places, theft or other violation of the city and state laws:"

Number cases examined 1,424
Discharged after examination 270

Punished in the work-house 330
Prosecuted or delivered to warrant 33
Fined or committed to the work-house until fine be paid 26
Penalties paid by owners or guardian 398
Runaways disposed of according to law 115
Delivered to the orders of the owners 252

The often riotous and troublesome population could in a measure be controlled in the city but it caused trouble just outside, as was the case on the outskirts of Columbia referred to above. The locality of most disturbance was on what was commonly known as "Charleston Neck," which is the long narrow strip of land extending some twelve miles back of the city between the Ashley and Cooper rivers. Driven from the city by a general tightening up of the municipal patrol the free negroes and insufficiently restrained slaves went just beyond the city limits to continue their disorder. The Charleston grand jury referred to this evil as early as 1744:

"We present as a grievance Negroes being allowed to go from Town into the Country under pretense of picking myrtle berries, etc., and who at the same time carry Rum and other Goods, to trade with Negroes in the Country, by which they are debauched and encouraged to steal and robb their masters of their corn, poultry and other provisions."

There was a further difficulty where there were very many free negroes, that slaves when caught by the patrol would endeavor to pass themselves as free persons. This was true of Charleston where according to the census of 1810 it was shown that there were 1,783 free negroes in the district. Hence a special act of 1823 by the General Assembly for the regulation of the patrol on "Charleston Neck" provided that any free negro might be whipped by the patrol when away from his home or his employer's premises unless he produced his "free papers," or convince the patrol of his freedom by other satisfactory proof. The act even goes further and declares that free negroes out of their own or their employer's premises after 9 p. m. without a ticket from their guardians would be liable to the same punishment meted out to a slave.

Owing to the difficulties incident to the proximity of the city this patrol of "the Neck" was often, if not for the greater part of the time, inefficient. The report on the proceedings of the city authorities in 1836 said that efforts to control the negroes in the city are futile, since they easily cross the boundary into "the Neck" where "the police is not and cannot be effective." A union of the two was thought desirable. A communication to the Charleston Courier of September 23, 1845, voiced the same feeling, pointing out the need of a guard-house. With an editorial deliverance from the Charleston Courier of April 25, 1834, must be dismissed the situation on "the Neck" peculiarly aggravating to the people of Charleston:

"On Charleston Neck it [i. e., the disorderliness] has become a serious evil, more particularly as it refers to the drunken gangs of drunken and riotous negroes pitching cents, and playing marbles, cursing and blaspheming in the vicinity of the ruinous and fatal sons of vice, the retail liquor shops, with which our city and neighborhood is so much infested. From these receptacles of iniquity they come forth, surcharged with the fumes of whiskey and segars in their mouths, staggering on their way, brawling and rioting totally regardless of decency and decorum. What has become of the Charleston Neck patrol?

There was a time when that patrol as a body, and in the respective districts, contributed much to suppress such malpractice and by its energy afforded protection, not merely to property but to the feelings of those who mostly have a claim upon their chivalry and honor, nor do we cease to look to the interposition of the Charleston Neck patrol as an auxiliary for enforcing the laws and of guarding the portions of the community against the continuance and further encroachments of habits and practices conducive to the awful and evitable consequences of immorality, vice and irreligion."

46

CHAPTER V. Punishment of Slaves

A great deal of the hostility to the institution of slavery came of the alleged cruelty to the slave; and much of this charge, it must be admitted, was well founded. However, the cruelty can, in some measure at least, be justified by the fact that nothing but the fear of a certain and severe physical punishment for misdoings could hold most slaves in check. The act of 1712 has often been pointed out as evidence of cruelty in its graduated scale of mutilations. However, these ideas were probably in large part a survival of English penal law. Furthermore this act was superseded in 1740, and although branding was not specifically forbidden until 1833, there is little that the writer has found in the way of mention in newspapers or elsewhere as evidence of anything other than whipping as a legal penalty for lesser offenses except a few instances of ear cropping. But there are abundant instances of private cruelty and unwarranted mistreatment if one wishes to dwell upon that side of slavery.

The plantation system involved many instances of harsh treatment at the hands of cruel masters and overseers. And it was on the large plantation that slavery could be seen at its worst, where the direct oversight of the master could not easily protect his interests in the humane treatment of the slaves. Neglect or failure properly to finish tasks, running away, theft, show of impudence and insolence, or violence to the other slaves with perhaps other small offenses was sure to call down upon an offender the justice of a wise manager or the wrath of a cruel overseer. In any instance it was not likely nor was it intended that any outside interference should be interposed so long as it could not be satisfactorily shown that the punishment led to a shortening of the slave's life or permanent injury, or as statute law would say, "extending to life or limb." The master or the manager under his authority was to be the sole judge of the grievousness of the offense and the number and severity of the strokes in whipping even if the punishment should disable the victim for a short time. The court records of cruelty to slaves discussed in a later chapter will suffice to illustrate the slightness of the probability that the master would be called to account. On the smaller farms, where the owners had the direct oversight, very little cruelty occurred. Many people could relate the lesser punishment meted out to their slaves as is recited in the humdrum diary of James Kershaw:

"1812, August 5, gave Jude a whipping for impudence." Offenses such as thieving or general disturbances were always punished with whipping, which was usually severe. Judge O'Neall had the following to say as to this method of punishment:

"The whippings inflicted by the sentence of courts trying slaves and free negroes are most enormous—utterly disproportioned to offenses—and should be prevented by all means in our power. In all cases where whipping is to be resorted to, I would limit the punishment by law, in all cases affecting both black and white, to forty, save one, and direct it to be inflicted in portions, and at considerable intervals of time. Thus mingling whipping and imprisonment together, and holding the rod suspended in the contemplation of the party, until the delay itself would be worse punishment than the infliction." Some instances of punishment may be mentioned. The following sentence was imposed by a court for negroes in Charleston upon a negro—presumably free—convicted of attempt to set fire to a private kitchen:

"Twenty lashes at Centre-Market, on 10th inst,—twenty lashes on 3rd of March—twenty on 24th of March, and twenty on 14th of April. Or if he so choose he may leave the state after the first whipping." Cuffy, a slave, received the following sentence for manslaughter of another slave at the hands of a similar tribunal : "Six weeks solitary confinement; three weeks upon the treadmill, and twenty lashes at three different times in the public market, at intervals of three weeks." A news note in the Rising Sun of April 27, 1859, gives this as the sentence imposed upon a negro for chicken stealing: "Nathan, a slave was tried and convicted for stealing chickens from a Mr.-, and sentenced to ninetyfive lashes. Peter, another slave, a witness in the case, being detected in several falsehoods and being believed to have an interest in said chickens, was sentenced to thirty lashes." The Darlington grand jury in its presentment at the fall term of court in 1852 called attention to their discovery in the dungeon of the jail of a slave named Scipio, who had been sentenced by a court for negroes to two years imprisonment and five hundred lashes;—undoubtedly, if there is not a mistake in transcribing the sentence, it was with the purpose of a distribution of the lashes—the request of the jury is that this be lessened since it would probably endanger the slave's life. Three negroes in Laurens district were convicted of assaulting a white man and sentenced to receive each five hundred lashes, evidently with a view to distributing them.

Transportation was another means of handling troublesome slaves. It has already been mentioned that being sold to a trader was held up as an evil from which the slave might well wish to escape. In 1833 a case arose involving the validity of a contract connected with a bill of sale to carry out of the state a certain slave. The court's opinion both as to the legality of such a contract and what of custom it involved is well worth quoting:

"Contracts of this sort are not unusual. The owners of slaves frequently send them off from amongst their kindred and associates as a punishment, and it is frequently resorted to as the means of separating a vicious negro amongst others exposed to be influenced and corrupted by his example. It is, therefore, common to require of the purchaser of such a negro, that he shall carry him out of the state. In such a contract there is nothing immoral, impolitic or illegal, and when, as in this case, it is founded on a valuable consideration there can be no doubt that it is binding." W. C. Bryant preserves to us one of the songs he heard sung by the negroes at a "corn shucking" while on a visit to South Carolina, probably at Barnwell. It is quoted to illustrate the fear they had of being sold into distant regions:

> "Johnny, come down de hollow.
> Oh hollow. De nigger-trader got he.
> Oh hollow. De speculator bought me.
> Oh hollow. I'm sold for silver dollars.
> Oh hollow. Boys, go catch de pony.
> Oh hollow. Bring him round de corner.
> Oh hollow. I'm goin' 'way to Georgia.
> Oh hollow. Boys, good-bye forever.
> Oh hollow."

The number of offenses, capital when committed by negroes, was greater than those in the case of white men. And the execution of the sentence in the case of negroes was probably more certain than in that of the whites. Any homicide of a white by a negro would probably be adjudged murder. It would be of little avail to sum up the capital offenses of the slave, for on the one side they appear far too few as specified in the statutes and on the other they would by no means cover all the offenses for which the extreme penalty could be imposed. For some offenses, particularly when they are repetitions, the fixing of the penalty is left to the court trying the case. One such will serve to illustrate. By the law of 1740 any slave presuming to strike a white person unless done at the command of his master or in defense of him, shall for the second or third offense suffer such punishment as the "court shall in their discretion think fitt, not extending to life or limb." For the third offense the penalty is death, or in case the slave "grievously wound or bruise any white person, though it shall be only the first offense, shall suffer death."

The act of 1751 authorized the court for the trial of slaves to commute the capital punishment required by law provided the circumstances under which the crime was committed should seem to warrant it. Also an act of 1834 gave the court discretion in any case not capital to substitute imprisonment for any other penalty not provided by law.

It seems that the slaveholding interest of South Carolina practically controlled all slave legislation during the period of its existence. A good illustration of this is the law which provided for the payment from the public treasury for every slave executed. This was in some form continued until the sixties. By the act of 1740 the maximum payment allowed was £200 but this was lowered to £40 in 1751. From 1800 to 1825 there appear among the acts of the Assembly the annual appropriations for executed slaves, the amount being uniformly $122.43. A compilation of these acts will also show how many legal hanging of negroes occurred. The largest number thus provided for was seven in 1812. For the other years the usual number was two or three, but in some years there were none. This argues well for the freedom of slaves from capital crime unless we may suppose that others were dealt with in a summary manner, or that no reimbursement was applied for.

For the next eighteen years no further account of payments for executed slaves appears, and it would seem that no such cases occurred, doubt even having arisen as to whether allowances for such compensation were legally in force, when in 1843 an act declared that such a law was in force and provided for the paying of the value of slaves executed during the four years just passed. This same legislature passed another act fixing the maximum penalty for an owner or overseer who concealed or conveyed away a slave charged with a capital offense at a fine of $1,000 and twelve months' imprisonment.

52

CHAPTER VI. Courts for the Trial of Negroes

There has been occasion for frequent references to courts for the trial of slaves and free negroes. We may now describe their organization and investigate their operation. The purpose of the early settlers in dealing with crimes committed by negroes seems to have been to make justice sure and swift. For example, in Charleston in 1733, on a Saturday afternoon, "a negro fellow" stole a horse from a boy who was riding him. The negro was caught on Sunday, tried by the tribunal for negroes on Monday and about noon on Tuesday paid the penalty on the gallows. None of the safeguards cherished by Englishmen, such as trial by jury, were thrown around the negro. It was a court given large discretion and unhampered by technicalities.

The courts as organized by the colonial act of 1690 remained the same with more or less unimportant modifications throughout the slavery regime. A fuller provision for them was made in the great negro law of 1740. Any justice of the peace being informed of the commission of a crime by a slave or free negro was immediately to despatch his constable to effect the arrest of the criminal, and forthwith to summon another justice nearest at hand together with not less than three nor more than five freeholders within three days, for the trial of the case. A quorum, which must consist of a justice and two freeholders, or of two justices and one freeholder, was sufficient to convict. The sentence was then to be fixed by the quorum according to law, and it will here be remembered that large discretion was allowed as to the penalties. There was, until very much later, no appeal from these courts.

We need not go outside the state to hear this system of trial condemned. A few quotations of official or representative character will suffice. The first is from Judge O'Neall, who had abundant opportunity to be acquainted with the workings of the court:

"The tribunal for the trial of slaves and free negroes is the worst system which could be devised. The consequence is, that the passions and prejudices of the neighborhood arising from a recent offense, enter into the trial, and often lead to the condemnation of the innocent." Another clearer statement is from the annual message of Governor Robert Y. Hayne to the legislature in 1833:

"In relation to the slaves my own experience and observation have convinced me that reform is imperiously called for. While rigid discipline should be enforced, the law ought at the same time to afford complete protection against injustice. The courts before which slaves must now be tried, for crimes of every description, are liable to be so arranged as to deprive them of an impartial trial.

"It is true that the moral sense of the community afford them, in general, protection from injustice, yet it is sufficient for us to know that the justices and freeholders are not unfrequently selected by the prosecutor, to perceive at once the liability of such a system to gross abuse. Capital offenses committed by slaves, involving the nicest questions of the law, are often tried by courts composed of persons ignorant of the law and left without the aid of counsel."

An editorial in the Charleston Mercury of Dec. 1, 1841, says that there ought to be

"an alteration of the laws for the trial of slaves for capital offences. . . . This is required not only for humanity's sake . . . but for the interests of the slaveholder. Not only the life of the slave but the property of the master are now in jeopardy from the ignorance and malice of unworthy magistrates, or perhaps a packed court of freeholders. In some neighborhoods the slave of a rich or popular man may be guilty with impunity, while the slave of a poor unpopular man is made to pay his life as the penalty of his master's unpopularity. Our policy as a slaveholding state requires that this species of property should be protected by a better system." Governor Richardson cited reasons in his annual message to the legislature of 1841 for believing that the usual actions of these courts were overhasty:

"The instances of awakened regret and contrition on the part of so many of these judicial tribunals, involving the interposition of executive clemency, to mollify or arrest their own hasty and often illegal convictions, are of frequent and ordinary occurrence."

And Governor Adams in 1855 said of the court:

"Their decisions are rarely in conformity with justice or humanity. I have felt constrained in a majority of the cases brought to my notice either to modify the sentence or to set it aside altogether." From these and other sources that could be cited the evils in the court as at first organized of which complaint was made may be classified as follows: First, for the trial of capital offenses the court as constituted did not even approximate jury trial, or fair selection. The first magistrate to whose attention the crime was called, no matter what his prejudices might be, constituted a sort of judge and foreman. This justice acting without limitation selected whom he would of resident freeholders to sit with him; and the verdict to convict did not have to be unanimous. Second, there was no opportunity to challenge (that is at first), either the presiding magistrate or the freeholders sitting with him. Nor was there any provision for the consideration of any ground of appeal. From the act of 1740 it would seem that guilt was to be presumed in the slave charged with crime unless the court found otherwise. Third, the master's or guardian's protection and defense of his ward was ill considered. It seems that it often occurred that slaves or free negroes were convicted without their masters or guardians being present or being allowed to be heard in person or through counsel. The Sumter grand jury in 1829 recommended the enactment of a law requiring, "the magistrate before whom a slave is charged with the commission of a crime or misdemeanor to give notice to the owner of the place where and the time when said slave is to be tried." This would seem to indicate the possibility of such conviction without the presence of the owner. Fourth, this gives the hint of another evil, that these trials were often held in secluded places, anywhere in the country where they were not exposed to the wholesome influence of publicity. Fifth, those who tried the case, including the magistrate, might be ignorant of the law, and often were likely to be swayed by prejudice or the present clamor of opinion.

This seems to be a quite sufficient indictment against the system. In the Charleston Courier of September 25, 1849, is a communication from a "Country Magistrate" which gives a clear, unconscious picture of a slave court. It is too long to quote in full, a summary will have to suffice: This magistrate, ten days after taking office, was informed of a case of poisoning, two negro women being charged with the crime. The new official had never seen a trial in a negro court and no lawyer was near. He proceeded to summon freeholders and another magistrate. One of the negroes was found to be plainly innocent. The other appeared to a majority of the court on circumstantial evidence to be guilty and was convicted by a vote of three to two of the court, but none thought the woman ought to be hanged, owing to the presence of the element of doubt. "But," it is added, "it was the unanimous opinion of the whole party—magistrates, freeholders, constables and visitors— that it could not be done legally"; that is that the extreme penalty could be inflicted or none. The negro was acquitted with the understanding that she would be sent out of the state, which the master consented to do. The quotation is sufficient to show the irregularity of the trial which was made a sort of community affair where a poll of those present was taken.

Another incident illustrative of the practical working and weakness of the system can be had from the record of a rehearing before Judge Wardlaw, a circuit court judge, at chambers in Abbeville, on error. It was the case of a slave condemned by a magistrate and freeholders' court to be hanged for burning a stable. The only effect of the rehearing, it may be remarked, was to set aside the verdict for the time being and grant a new trial by another magistrate and freeholder's court which would observe the proper procedure. On a rehearing before a superior court (provisions amending the old regulations which will be discussed in a few paragraphs further down) the record was the only evidence submitted. Judge Wardlaw set aside the verdict on ten enumerated grounds, the most important of which were that the records did not show: that the owner had been duly notified; that the freeholders were residents of the district or that they had been properly summoned; that the witnesses had been sworn; that anybody had been heard in the negro's defence; that any definite time for the execution had been fixed; nor, lastly, "that there was a distinct statement in writing of the offense for which the prisoner was put on trial, to which the testimony was annexed." Of this last objection the court says further: "An accurate statement of the offense is required, as well by the principles of justice as by the positive words of the law. Time . . . should be stated . . . place also; and the essential ingredients of the offense which contains them, or by separate enumerations." Even supposing these objections to have been merely technical errors, it shows a reckless disregard of justice to the accused man of color. But it gives us some idea of the practical workings of one of these courts.

Now the remedies proposed by governors, grand juries, editors and legal writers may be summed up as follows: First, a limited form of jury trial with a fair number of challenges by the owner or guardian without cause, and a greater number for cause. Second, that appeal be allowed to some superior court, the most feasible the circuit court, on an abstract of the case. Third, that the trial be conducted publicly at the court-house seat in the district. Fourth, that sometime between the verdicts and execution for capital offenses be allowed to elapse to afford an opportunity for a review of the case by the Chief Executive with a view to the possible need for executive clemency.

An unlimited jury trial could hardly be expected though so loudly and from some places apparently so urgently called for. The Charleston Mercury of November 30, 1855, in an editorial comment on Governor Adams' recommendations, points out the possibility of abuse in the owner's interest by requiring a unanimous verdict for conviction and hence justice might fail.

While not all, indeed only a few and these very much limited, suggestions became laws, it would be surprising if the recommendations did not have effect in the direction of some modification and liberalizing of the trial system. Section 5 of an act concerning negroes passed in 1831, gave the master, guardian or agent the right of challenge for cause of any persons selected to try a slave or free negro deemed a hardship, certain points more or less public might be designated by law. News note in the Southern Patriot, Dec. 11, 1845, says that a bill giving the owner the privilege of changing the venue of the trial of one of his slaves accused of crime from his own community to the court-house passed the lower house of the General Assembly in that year but was thrown out in the Senate on a technicality, for a capital offense, the presiding magistrate being the judge of the validity of the cause. And the next section prohibited the trial of a slave for any offense in the absence of the master or the master's agent, or until reasonable notice to the master of the place and time of the trial and the offense charged had been given.

In 1832 a special act for the trial of negroes in the city of Charleston required a unanimous verdict for the conviction of a free negro.

An act of 1833 gave the right to the accused of appeal to the circuit court from a negro court for any slave or free negro convicted of a capital offense. The circuit judge was to review the case from a report sent up by the negro court. It seems, however, that the most that the superior court could do was to grant a new trial, from which all of those who sat in the first trial were to be excluded from participating. In 1817 another legal process had been resorted to in Union district where the judge had upon petition entered a rule upon a court of magistrates and freeholders to show cause why they should not be restrained from carrying into effect a verdict of their court upon a slave. Later the complaint was withdrawn and the rule dismissed. Under the provisions of this act Judge Bay in circuit set aside a verdict of a court of magistrates and freeholders in 1835 in a case where a free negro had been sentenced to death for the murder of a slave. The grounds upon which he acted were that the oath had not been properly administered and that magistrates not resident in the district in which the crime was committed were allowed to sit in the case. In 1858 three negroes in Laurens district, who had been convicted for assaulting a white man and had been sentenced to be hanged, were granted a new trial by Judge O'Neall on the ground that the act was not "malicious."

Another salutary measure was that, if requested, the negro court had to allow sufficient time between the finding of a verdict in a capital case and its execution to give the governor ample time to review it for executive clemency.

The laws of the slave and negro courts did not provide for the keeping of any record of the trial—only another evidence of the irregularity of their procedure . . . and even when the record was submitted for review by a superior court the facts were sometimes not all set out, as shown by the Abbeville appeal case. Hence it has not been the good fortune of the writer to find any official papers bearing on the manner in which they were conducted. It is probable that this court was not often resorted to except for the punishment of capital offenses though it had jurisdiction in smaller cases as well. There were likely other methods more summary with which smaller offenses like petty theft could be dealt. A good whipping by an outsider when the offense was clear and the evidence unquestioned would probably have been acquiesced in by the master.

60

CHAPTER VII. Relations Between Whites and Blacks

To the slave was extended the protection of the law in so far as enactment and interpretation were concerned. The colonial act of 1690 provided a penalty of three months' imprisonment for a master who should unduly injure his slave unless the injury was inflicted in an effort to prevent his running away from due chastisement. By the law of 1712 a master was to be fined £30 for the murder of his own slave if for "bloody mindedness." If the slave was owned by another, the murderer was to be liable to owner for the value of the slave in addition to a fine of £25. An act passed in 1722 provided that: "whereas there is reason to suspect that slaves do run away from a want of sufficient allowance of provisions" the justices of the peace should be empowered to fine the owner £50 for failure to provide sufficient clothing and food for his slaves; a sum larger, it will be observed, than for his murder. If he "do run away" he would become a menace to the neighbors. By the act of 1740 the heaviest penalty that could be inflicted for the murder of a slave by a white person was £700, or if the defendant should be unable to pay the fine, seven years' imprisonment at hard labor could be substituted. But if the deed was committed in sudden heat of passion the penalty was to be a fine of £10. For lesser cruelty to a slave the fine was £10 and for not providing sufficient clothing it was £3. About 1807 a slave owner in Charleston had one of his slaves to chop off the head of another slave. Judge Withers, in passing sentence on the white man, expresses regret that the penalty for the murder of a slave under such revolting circumstances was so light.

An agitation for making more severe the penalty for the murder of a slave was begun sometime about the opening of the new century. If we may believe a communication to The Times (Charleston) of June 2, 1806, negro homicides were occurring frequently. This article makes the point that the penalty for killing a negro was less than for stealing him. In the fall of the same year a member of the Legislature gave notice of his intention to introduce a bill with this purpose in view, but nothing was done. However, a committee was appointed under joint resolution of both houses of the General Assembly to recommend changes in the criminal code after deliberation during the recess. This committee among other things said:

"But your committee beg leave further to report that in the opinion of the said joint committee it will be proper to alter and increase the present punishments of the crime of manslaughter and murdering a slave." A proposed bill accompanied the report, but no such law was passed. In 1808, as was then customary, parts of the presentments of grand juries of the various districts recommending certain legislation were laid before the lawmaking body by their respective delegations. From the Kershaw grand jury in 1808 came the complaint that the existing laws to prevent the murder of slaves were inadequate. The following description of conditions by the Charleston grand jury in 1816 carries with it the seal of official authority:

"The grand jury further present as a serious evil the many instances of Negro Homicide, which have been committed within the city for many years. The parties exercising unlimited control as masters and mistresses, in the indulgence of the malignant and cruel passions in the barbarous treatment of slaves, using them worse than beasts of burden, and thereby bringing on the community, the state and the city the contumely and opprobrium of the civilized world."

At the fall term of court in Darlington in 1816 the trial jury in the case of a prisoner charged with negro stealing returned this unusual verdict:

"Guilty. On the determination of the case of the said we, the jury recommend him to mercy, believing the crime of stealing a negro is not more deserving of death than the murdering which only subjects to fine and imprisonment." Notwithstanding the jury's recommendation the prisoner was sentenced to be executed. The Southern Patriot of Dec. 1, 1819, also contains a letter from a correspondent urging the death penalty for murder of a slave by a white person.

These are sufficient to show that there was a fairly general feeling that the murder of a slave by anybody ought to be made a capital offense. But like all reforms it had to abide its time. In 1820 the feeling was sufficiently prevalent for Governor Geddes to call attention in his annual message to the inadequacy of the penalty as it then was, saying that it has held us up to the world as being inhuman because "a slave being deprived of his natural right of self-defense against a white man the killing of him by the latter receives from the circumstances additional aggravation." But the message was answered by no enactment. According to McCrady action was finally precipitated by a well-known case of the murder of a runaway slave by his master. The lawmaking body at last heeded the demands of progress and passed in 1821 the necessary act making the murder of a slave punishable with death. If the deed should be committed in sudden heat and passion the penalty was a fine of $500 and six months' imprisonment.

The effect of this enactment was interpreted by the Court of Appeals in 1834 as follows:

"This change I think made a most important alteration in the law of his [the slave's] personal protection. It in a criminal point of view elevated slaves from chattels personal to human beings in the peace of society." A still broader interpretation is given in 1852 by the same court:

"The battery of a slave is equally with the battery of his owner a breach of the peace; and the license of the plaintiff to beat his slave can no more be pleaded in justification than the license of the plaintiff to beat himself."

But in this connection it must be remembered that the master had an almost unlimited right of correcting his slave and that if the slave offered resistance he would thereby commit a crime. It was thus stated by the highest tribunal in 1831:

"To a master, by the common law of this state, a slave owes passive obedience; to enforce it the master has the right of correction, and if while exercising this right, the slave should kill his master, he would be guilty at common law; . . . and his aiders and abettors being present would be guilty of the same offense."

The question naturally arises, how well was the law against slave murder enforced? For this information we may secure some light from the criminal court records in the offices of the clerks of court in the various counties.

Many of these have been destroyed or are in a bad state of preservation. But sufficient more or less fragmentary records are available to form some idea of the prevalence of the crime and the checking influence of the courts.

Before we come to these we can refer to a few more or less noteworthy examples of the convictions of white persons for the murder of slaves. One was the execution of a white man in Marlborough district in 1852 for the murder of a female slave. Another conviction was in Chester district, where a white man was convicted in the Sessions Court in 1834. It was appealed to the higher court but the verdict of the lower court was reaffirmed. In the Pendleton Messenger of December 9, 1838, appears a statement by Governor P. M. Butler, setting forth the reasons why he refused clemency to a youth in Richland district who had wantonly killed a slave, although a largely signed petition had been before him praying for the mercy of the Executive. The account does not state whether the sentence was finally carried to execution or not, but it probably was. Still another in Colleton district was the case of the "Broxton Bridge Horror," where two white men, one the son of the owner of the slave and the other a white assistant, who together, on capturing the slave after his having run away, put him to death by torture extending over a day and a night. The Colleton case and the Marlborough cases were revolting in the extreme. In the former case the militia were on duty at the execution by the Governor's orders to prevent any attempt at rescue.

The criminal records of Sumter district are practically complete from 1827 to 1854. During this period of nearly thirty years there were eleven bills charging murder of slaves by white persons placed in the hands of the grand jury by the solicitor. In the case of three the grand jury reported "no bill." As to one of these three they reported after the "no bill" this explanation: "bad treatment, not intentional murder." Another bill at the same term of court was returned against the same person charging the murder of a slave—whether it was for the same offense or on another separate charge does not appear. The prisoner was arraigned, tried and acquitted. In the other cases, six were tried and found "not guilty." Of the remaining two, one pleaded guilty, but no sentence is recorded; while the last received a verdict "true bill on second count," no sentence being entered.

The first slave case recorded in an old fragmentary record under date of 1812 in the clerk of court's office at Darlington is an "indictment for killing a negro," the defendant on the following year being found "not guilty." A case returned "true bill" appears in 1825 but no further trace of its final disposal could be found. From 1840 to 1861 there were three indictments for slave murder recorded. They were disposed of as follows: for the first a verdict, "guilty, self-defense," is the return, meaning probably justifiable homicide; the second was found not guilty, the indictment during the progress of the trial having been changed from murder to "murder in sudden heat and passion"; opposite the third is recorded "not arrested." This latter case the grand jury took up and presented the sheriff for non-performance of duty. Later the records show that a true bill had been found against the person in the last case, but he probably escaped justice in the end, as no further record in reference to him appears.

The Williamsburg county records are fragmentary down to 1840, and are more or less confused and crudely transcribed, and the dockets often fail to show whether the cases were acted upon even by the grand jury. However, in such records as are preserved from 1817 to 1860 ten bills for the murder of slaves by whites are entered. Of these "true bills" are returned in only four cases with no convictions. In the other six cases there appears "struck off" or no further mention.

In Newberry district, from 1840 to 1860, there were five charges for slave murder entered. One defendant pleaded guilty in 1855 but no record as to the sentence is available. The other four came to trial and the defendants were acquitted.

In the records of Kershaw county, dating back as far as 1789, though those for a period of twenty-three years are missing and those preserved are otherwise unsatisfactory, we find six persons charged with murder of negroes; the defendant in one case was sentenced to be hanged for another offense; in another case a "no bill" was returned by the grand jury; in two instances a "true bill' is twice returned for each case but no trial appears to have taken place; in two cases the defendants were put upon their trial and acquitted. In these six cases is included one in 1806 under the charge of "burning a negroe"; it was on this case that the grand jury refused to bring an indictment.

For Marlborough district the sessions records contain the one already mentioned (p. 70); only three cases of slave murder by whites besides in two of which the investigation led to "no bill"; in another, in

1819-before the murder of a slave was made a capital offense—the trial jury found the defendant guilty of manslaughter and the following sentence is recorded: "360 old currency—to remain in custody until fine and both are paid."

The records of Union district from 1804 to 1860 have five cases of slave murder recorded. In the first, in 1804, the defendant was convicted and fined $100 and the costs of the suit. Two of the others are found not guilty; in one no indictment was returned by the grand jury; in another case no mention of its final disposal is made.

From the available records of Spartanburg district from 1806 to 1860 there are four persons charged with slave murder. One was found guilty in 1815, the sentence being "that he remain in jail until he pays the fine of seven hundred pounds of old currency." In 1816 two white men were charged with the murder of the same negro, the verdict of the jury being, "We find the defendants guilty of killing by undue correction," and the sentence was "that they pay the sum of three hundred and fifty pounds old currency each and to stand committed until the fine is paid." In another, in 1818, the defendant pleaded guilty but no sentence is recorded. The last, in 1849, was nolle prossed.

The indexed criminal records of Laurens county extending back to 1801 contain nine bills charging murder of slaves by whites. The defendants in two of the cases were found "guilty on the second count," the sentence in one instance being $500 and six months' imprisonment, but in the other no sentence was found recorded. In a third case the defendant was found guilty of manslaughter and sentenced to a fine of $500 and imprisonment for three weeks. In a fourth case the only record left is that opposite it in the docket, "guilty and sentenced." Of the remaining five cases one was struck from the docket, while the other four were brought to trial and the defendants acquitted.

Unless it escaped the search of the writer or appeared on an unpreserved record, no case of slave murder against whites was brought in Greenville from 1806 to 1860. By the census of 1810 there were five whites for every negro in this district, and in 1850 there were three whites for every negro.

There is nothing in any of these records to show what relation the aggressor sustained to the slave, whether master, owner's overseer, or purely an outsider. It is a reasonable conjecture, however, that in case the majority of offenses had been committed by outsiders or even by an overseer, more convictions would have been secured from a more vigorous prosecution of the charge. In the Southern Chronicle of Aug. 26, 1846, was the notice of a reward of $100 offered by the Governor for the apprehension of one who had killed a slave belonging to another person. Speaking generally, if the deed was committed by a person who had property it is more than likely that a civil action would have been brought by the owner, and unless it were a flagrant outrage probably no criminal action at all would be taken. In any case there was every advantage of the benefit of a doubt given a white man who murdered a slave—the disparity of racial condition was so great. It would then be difficult to secure the conviction of a white man under any circumstances. The property interest of the master could not have failed to be a source of protection to his slave. The property interest in some measure at least protected the slave from violence at the hands of the master himself and caused the latter to secure overseers who he thought would not likely offend along this line. But increased difficulty would be encountered in bringing to justice the slaveowner who even unjustly took the life of his slave. The expense and trouble of the prosecution of a person who had more or less of wealth and social prestige as a defense was great. The evidence would likely be scant—only negroes, if anybody, would probably be witnesses and they could not testify against a white person. And then the master could very easily enter the plea that it occurred as the result of resistance on the part of the slave to lawful correction. Here the matter in all probability most often ended. Where death resulted from cruelty, unless it were sudden and violent and its inhumanity was apparent, it is extremely doubtful whether the case ever came to the attention of the courts at all. However, the Laurensville Herald of February 5, 1858, has a strong editorial condemning cruelty to slaves and uses as an illustration the case of a white man who had caused the death of his slaves by ill treatment. It appears that a committee of citizens in the community had waited upon this particular slaveowner and demanded that he leave the community at once, which he did. After relating this incident (of a kind rarely committed to print in ante-bellum days) the editor gives full approval of the irregular proceeding of this master's neighbors.

What has just been said as to the probabilities of a white person taking the life of a slave is applicable to the question of the humane treatment of the slave by the whites. The criminal dockets of the nine counties before mentioned yield more data on this point than on the former. The law of 1740 provided no higher penalty than a fine of £100 for any cruelty to a slave, even mutilation and loss of member not endangering life. By an act of 1841 the unlawful whipping of a slave was punishable by a maximum penalty of a fine of $500 or six months' imprisonment. But this act made it quite clear that exception was to be made in the case of the owner or overseer, or one to whom the slave had offered insult or insolence. To make this "lawful" correction entirely permissible an act was passed in 1858 in which it was clearly set forth that the master did have the right to administer such punishment as was necessary in the proper discipline and control of his slaves. The sessions dockets of the courts have a number of charges entered, such as "unlawfully whipping a slave," "cruelty to slave," "assault and battery on a slave," "unlawfully beating a slave." On the available sessions docket of Sumter county from 1827 to 1854 there are entered thirteen such cases. Two defendants pleaded guilty; five were convicted but no recorded sentence appears except for one where the fine is $1. Six of these cases are either dropped or without further record.

In Darlington district for twenty years, from 1840 to 1861, there were twenty-three such cases. Two came to trial, one in 1847 and one in 1848, and verdicts of guilty rendered with fines of $25 and $62.50 respectively imposed. Three more cases were tried and guilt established but no record occurs of any penalties imposed. The remaining eighteen are returned "no bill"; either the defendants were acquitted, or the record fails to show any further action in the case.

In Williamsburg district from 1840 to 1860 twelve such cases appear on the docket, of which the record shows no conviction and only six reach the stage of "true bill" and these are struck from the record later.

In Newberry district from 1842 to 1860 there were only seven such indictments with convictions recorded in only two of them but with no penalties attached.

There is no record of any indictment being brought against a white person in Kershaw district for cruelty to slaves.

It is different in Marlborough district, where negroes were apparently well protected. Nine such cases appear on the docket, three being brought at intervals against the same person. In only two cases did the grand jury fail to indict and in each of the remaining seven convictions were secured. The fines were $20 and $25 except in the case of one defendant who pleaded guilty and the fine was fixed at $1. Imprisonment was the sentence in three cases—in one for a term of one week, in another for ten days and in another three months. The grand jury in 1847 presented the same person referred to above as having later been indicted three times for cruelty as follows: "For beating, tearing with dogs and otherwise cruelly treating two negroes (namely Rina and Julia), the property of Mrs. , and disturbing the neighborhood with riotous and disorderly conduct." Similar presentments of cruelty were made by the grand jury in 1849. Again, in 1855 an owner was "presented" "for not feeding and clothing his negroes."

In Union district twenty-two cases for cruelty to slaves were considered. The defendant in one case pleaded guilty; in only four others were convictions reached, though the record in none of the cases could be found.

In Spartanburg district, according to the available records, five cases of cruelty to slaves are noted, in only one of which a conviction is reached, the sentence being one month's imprisonment.

In Greenville district ten cases charging bad treatment of slaves were brought up. One case in 1856 is marked "settled." In only three of the others is there a conviction secured, the defendant in one being fined $1; in another the sentence is a fine of $20 and four months' imprisonment; in the last no sentence appears.

In Laurens district three such cases were brought up; one was returned by the grand jury "no bill"; in another the fine was $5; the last, apparently an unwarranted disturbance of negroes probably at religious worship by white persons, for the charge also includes disturbance of religious worship, the defendant was fined $20 and imprisonment one month.

In a letter to The Rising Sun (Newberry) of April 20, 1859, from Greenville, which was included in his judicial circuit, Judge O'Neall says that in the court then just closed quite a large number of the cases on the docket were "trespass for hitting or beating a slave."

In this connection three phases of the subject should be noted: First, as already stated, in the case of the murder of a slave the master's property interest in the slave in a large measure protected him from the outsider. It is probable that the cases of convictions noted may have been from outside aggressors caused by a prosecution by the master. We must think of the owner as standing ready to punish by legal means any person who should presume unprovoked to punish or whip any of his slaves. But while it was not lawful perhaps there was a sort of unwritten law among the white population that a negro caught stealing could be whipped with impunity; and it sometimes occurred that on a person's making complaint to the master of theft by the latter's slave, though the complainant was not a slaveholder, the master would turn the slave over to him for castigation. The master would possibly find this outside correction a means of checking the evil of the slave's leaving his cabin at night. Such cases would arise—as we know one in Newberry did—from undue interference of the patrol.

In the next place a difficulty in such prosecutions arose in securing evidence. No person of color could testify against a white person. Thus it was that only exceptional cases based largely on circumstantial evidence were brought. This difficulty applies also in the case of the murder of a slave. In one of the records just referred to, a case in 1844, in which all the papers are preserved, it is shown by the affidavits of white persons that the person charged with the murder, together with another white man, caught the negro stealing potatoes, that they were seen to disappear in a swamp forcing the negro along with them with a rope around his neck, beating him all the while. A few days afterwards the negro was found dead in the swamp as a result probably of such treatment. Notwithstanding the probability that there was a strong prosecution by the master, the defendants were acquitted.

The last point to be noted is the undoubted necessity of more or less severe corporal punishment to keep the slaves under control. Hence the master and his overseer were given by law and public sentiment considerable latitude. Only the most flagrant violations of humanity were ever likely to find their way into the courts, and even then the accused had the decided advantage of every possible doubt.

In other words, the plantation was a sort of governmental unit as to police control of the slave, and to its head, the slaveowner, was given in large measure the sovereign management of its affairs under certain restrictions.

Similarly, in a series of articles on "Prospects of Southern Agriculture," in DeBow's Review is this statement:

"The cultivator of the soil is a ruler. The slaveowner is more—he is to a certain extent necessarily a despot. He makes the regulations that govern his plantation and he executes them. It is true he is amenable to public opinion for his acts and any flagrant outrage is visited by the laws; but there are a thousand incidents of plantation life concealed from public view which the law cannot reach."

72

CHAPTER VIII. Trading with Slaves

One of the most frequent charges with reference to negroes noted on the criminal dockets of the sessions court is "trading with slaves," "unlawful trading with slaves," or "unlawful trafficking with slaves." It is not difficult to understand the reason for the enactment of laws prohibiting with more or less severe penalties any person from trading with a slave. If unrestricted it would have meant the indiscriminate petty stealing of farm produce, corn, cotton, rice, fowls, eggs and almost anything else by the slaves, which opportunity might offer. This they would sell to the unscrupulous for a pittance that would afford a sort of income which their condition otherwise prevented securing. The selling of articles to slaves for money or in barter was also prohibited for the same reason. The laws against slave trading, however, were one of the best illustrations of laws that are put on the statute books to be used as occasion demanded. They were systematically disregarded by farmer and merchant when the slave was known to be reliable, or when he was sent on an errand to make a purchase. The enactments were intended to reach the person who took advantage of the illegal traffic for the sake of the profit when he necessarily knew it was done without the consent of the master. "The negro trader" was regarded in much the same light, though in a greatly modified sense, as the person who stole slaves. By virtue of his business, he became an enemy of his fellows and a menace to the established order of society, a disturber of the peace of the community. Trading with slaves carried with it a social stigma that hampered one's reputation. "He is a negro trader" was one of the most disagreeable terms that could be applied to a white man. Some merchants who did a small business carried on this kind of illicit bartering, for it yielded large profits as a reward so long as his dealings were undetected and so long as he did not incur the positive hatred of the community. Pedlers were often looked upon askance because they sold to slaves.

When a slave appeared in the broad open day with money and offered to make a purchase it seems that reliable merchants sold to him, taking the offer of money as evidence that he was making the purchase for the master or at least with the master's knowledge and consent, although strictly this was unlawful trading making the person so engaged liable to the penalties of the act. The provisions of the laws prohibited any trading with a slave unless he produced a written permit from his master or the overseer in whose charge he was. The Charleston Courier of June 5, 1816, comments editorially on a case recently decided by the court, that any acceptance of money from a slave without a ticket in trade is unlawful trafficking; it says: "The decision is of some importance to retailers and most of the trading part of the community. It has been found a general practice with them, we are informed, to take money from slaves without the owner's permission to trade. The money has been regarded as the permit. And unless where the largeness of the sum has excited suspicion, that the slave has not come fairly by it, the money offered has been rarely refused. It will now be seen that this is illegal: and that whosoever receives to the value of one cent from a slave without the written permission of the owner or manager violates a public law and subjects himself to a penalty of $200.

"The law was passed for the benefit of slaveholders. They must not find fault then when they send a slave to a shop, that he is sent home without the article wanted because seven pence cannot be received without a ticket from the master. Ye owners of slaves, hereafter keep your ink by you or go yourselves for what you want. The shopkeeper, who does not require this of you is unjust to himself." Trading and selling by negroes—free negroes as well as slaves—was looked upon as an evil at an early period because it afforded encouragement to theft. The Charleston grand jury several times called attention to it. The following section of their presentment in 1737 will serve as an illustration:

"We present as a grievance the practice of negroes buying and selling wares in the streets of Charleston, whereby stolen goods may be concealed and afterwards Vended undiscovered, as also negroes going in boats and canoes up the country trading with negroes in a clandestine way." But none of the laws up to 1796 were severe. They were enacted more with a view to reaching and punishing the slave than punishing the white man who became his accomplice by trading with him; for example the act of 1751 provided for only a fine of forty shillings for unlawful trading by a white person.

Apparently it was soon realized that more severe measures must be resorted to and that the slave from his inherent racial thieving tendencies would take the risk of a whipping so long as there was someone who would lend his aid by becoming the purchaser of his stolen goods. The act of 1796 made the maximum penalty for trading with a slave without a permit $200. But this seems to have been an insufficient deterrent—indeed, increasing of penalties appears to have had but little effect. Hence in 1817 another act was passed which recited the reason for its enactment as follows :

"Whereas it is found by experience that the penalties heretofore imposed on shopkeepers and other traders who deal with negroes without permission of their owners, are insufficient, and have not answered the ends intended . . . ." This statute imposed a maximum fine of $1,000 and twelve months' imprisonment on any shopkeeper or his clerk who should buy from a slave without his master's permit, "corn, rice, peas, or other grain, bacon, flour, tobacco, indigo, cotton, hay or other article whatsoever." The person trading with the slave was required to retain the written permit as a warrant for his trading. In 1834 another law prohibited the purchase of the usual farm produce from a slave "either with or without a permit" from his master under the same penalties as provided in the act of 1817. When a shopkeeper was charged with having received from a slave any such articles the burden of proof to the contrary rested with the accused. The Charleston Courier, in a lengthy editorial on April 18, 1835, says that dealers thought that this latter law would seriously interfere with their business, but the opinion of the editor was that it would not interfere with traffic that was understood not to be repugnant to the interests of the community but to reach the liquor dealer; his popular interpretation of the new law is worth quoting:

"Under the former law the usage has been to sell the necessaries and innocent conveniences of life to the slave without a permit. The new law contains nothing to render this usage more unlawful than it was before, and we can see no good reason why it cannot still be innocently indulged in. The main object of the old law was to lessen the danger of the depredation on the property of owners by making it highly penal to purchase from or traffic with their slaves. The main object of the new law is to prevent slaves from being corrupted in their habits and ruined in their constitutions by the use of intoxicating liquors." But these two acts failed effectually to check the unlawful and aggravating traffic. The Sumter grand jury had said in 1828:

"The grand jury of Sumter district present as a grievance the permission to shopkeepers and others to trade with negroes after dark, even with a ticket from their owners, and submit the propriety of the passage of a law by the Legislature, imposing a heavy penalty upon anyone convicted of trading with a negro after dark or on the Sabbath even with a permit from the owner." This same body again in 1834 said, in speaking of negro trading, that it "has become the chief object of pursuit and the chief source of gain" of many and they appealed to every good citizen to contribute his exertion to put it down. The following notice appearing in the Rising Sun (Newberry) of Jan. 18, 1860, shows the determination of one slaveowner to stop unlawful trading:

"I will give $500 for proof to convict for anyone buying pork, corn, fodder or any other produce from my negroes without a special order from me in my own handwriting."

The following open letter to farmers by "A Citizen," published in the Farmer and Planter of July, 1857, shows the kind of small trafficking that is winked at and soon shades into the irresponsible and menacing trade:

"Let me call your attention to the liberties now allowed to negroes. Who thinks it necessary to ask for a ticket or permit to trade? Just give a fellow some chickens, a stolen turkey, or a bushel of corn, and let him pace the streets and see how many and how respectable are the purchasers. This I adduce as the evidence of a loose rein, yes, an uncurbed privilege. Constant usage for some time has rendered it common and unseemingly justifiable, but this will lead to ruin if not arrested. Let a white man go to town and offer a few bushels of potatoes for sale and negroes bring them here every day at such and such a price. I am not talking of this matter as a pecuniary consideration but alone to show the widespread ruin that awaits us as slaveholders, unless this thing is checked and our negroes are brought to chalk a line, and the only means available is in our prompt action with the offending. If you will not inflict upon them the punishment provided by our laws, then inflict that one of caste and disgrace. Make him feel his inferiority, and feel it, too, in his pocket, the surest road to the heart of such offenders; better this than the ruin that awaits you in your present course."

The magazine then comments editorially on the communication as follows:

"The following communication is received just at a time, owing to local circumstances, we feel strongly inclined to put a stop to a prevailing practice that is having a bad effect on our slaves. Custom we know has done much toward tolerating the practice of buying from slaves, but we think it high time to put a stop to the custom. We never could see any more propriety in one man buying poultry, eggs, etc., from a negro than in another buying meat, corn, or other products not usually made by the slave. The latter practice is much less frequent than the former.

"Also, turn over a new leaf with your overseer, exact a greater degree of vigilance and use the same yourself. . . . It is indispensable for the welfare of all concerned."

The two selections above were copied in the Laurensville Herald with the following comment by that paper:

"We honestly believe that more injury is done to the slaves by trafficking with them than in any other way.

"We earnestly call upon our housekeepers to set their faces against trafficking with negroes without permission from their owners. One of the greatest complaints made by our friends in the country against the village is, that they will traffick with their negroes, thereby encouraging them to steal and giving them the means of buying liquor and to engage in gambling. The fact is, we look upon it as a very dishonest transaction." One thing which encouraged the trading, indeed, made much of it necessary, was the humane custom of allowing to the slave a garden, or cotton or corn patch to be cultivated after work hours or after a task had been finished, or the privilege of raising poultry, the products of which the slave was allowed to dispose of as he might see fit. This made some selling by the slave of his products necessary, and the frequency of such a custom caused owners to neglect to furnish the legal permit.

The custom of this side farm found its way into Grayson's Hireling and Slave: "Calm in his peaceful home the slave prepares His garden spot, and plies his rustic cares; The comb and honey that his bees afford. The eggs in ample gourd compactly stored. The pig, the poultry, with a chapman's art. He sells or barters at the village mart, Or at the master's mansion, never fails An ampler price to find and readier sales." Often the produce was bought by the master or sold at the market by him to overcome this very objection of unlawful traffic. The serious objection to this encourage merit of the slave's thrift lay in the fact that it helped to cover up his thefts from other people in the community. Furthermore the objection could be made that it put money in his hands for evil purposes, buying liquor and gambling. This latter objection does not appear to have been much advanced, since probably the owner's interest in keeping the slaves up to the highest point of industrial efficiency would cause him to refuse such privileges to his slaves if they were taken advantage of in this way.

A large majority of the cases relating to slavery that appeared on the dockets of the sessions courts were charges against white persons for trading with slaves. Anything more than the briefest summary of the cases tried and how disposed of would give but little light on the subject. But these dockets will be suggestive as to the proportion of the convictions and the penalties imposed.

In Williamsburg district the available dockets from 1817 to 1860 show that about 35 per cent, of the indictments reached conviction. The highest penalty imposed was in 1856 when a fine of $100 and two months' imprisonment was the sentence.

The records of Darlington district show convictions in about 40 per cent, of the indictments. The penalties range from one month's imprisonment and a fine of $20 to six months and a fine of $250. The fines and terms of imprisonment are evidently arranged with a view to suiting the punishment to the relative financial condition of the convicts; some are given a term of imprisonment with no fine while others are given from one to three months' term with a heavier fine.

In Sumter district, where it seems that for some reason the law was better enforced, the records from 1827 to 1860 show that there were convictions in about 48 per cent of the cases brought for negro trading. For a period of four years, 1827-1831, the authorities appear to have laid a heavy hand on the unlawful traders, there being ten convictions out of a total of fourteen cases. The heaviest sentence was a fine of $500 and four months' imprisonment—the fine was "remitted," however, by the governor. In five of the other cases the fine was $200 with varying terms of imprisonment. The effect was noticeable; for a decade the percentage of indictments for trading with slaves was unusually small.

In Kershaw district the records show convictions in about 38 per cent, of the indictments. The journal is very unsatisfactory, often stating the mere fact of conviction with no sentence attached. In two cases, in 1808 and 1809, the penalty was a fine of $200 and costs; in another in 1845 the penalty was six weeks' imprisonment.

For Marlborough district the percentage of convictions is 43. The highest punishment imposed was six months' imprisonment and a fine of $200; the smallest penalty was a fine of $50; in another case it was fixed at $50 and one month's imprisonment.

The records of Greenville district from 1817 to 1860 reveal convictions in only about 20 per cent, of the cases tried. The heaviest penalty imposed was in 1843 and was two months' imprisonment and a fine of $100; in another the sentence was one month's imprisonment and a fine of one cent. The large percentage of women charged is noticeably higher than in those of any other district visited. Convictions in 39 per cent, of the cases brought in Spartanburg district from 1806 to 1860 were reached. The penalties imposed range from two weeks' imprisonment and a fine of $1 to five months and $100. There seems at no time to have been any long sustained effort to break up the evil as was the case in Sumter district.

Union district presents, for its population, a very large array of indictments for negro trading and succeeded in convicting only 30 per cent, of the persons so charged in the period, 1815-1860. The sentences recorded are the usual ones, ranging not higher than a fine of $100 and the usual term of a few months' imprisonment.

The docket in Laurens district shows nothing more than ordinary in the prosecution of offenders against the law prohibiting whites from trading with negroes. Convictions were secured in about 42 per cent, of the cases brought. The sentence in one case was a fine of $500; in another, $200 and three months' imprisonment; while in another it was as small as a fine of $1 and one month's imprisonment.

Probably in quite a number of these cases cited the charge was compromised by the persons concerned, thus making the indictments and convictions fewer than they would have been. The cases appearing on the dockets do not give even a comparatively approximate idea of the number of offenses as the cases of stealing of slaves do. Many an illicit trader was never brought to justice because of the expense and trouble as compared with the value of the stolen articles trafficked in and because of lack of evidence sufficient to convict.

This matter of securing the evidence necessary to conviction was one of the greatest difficulties to be overcome. Where illicit trading was suspected the master would often send his slave with instructions to effect a bargain while he was near in hiding. The Constitutional Court held in 1819 that trading with a slave in the presence of his master, the latter failing to sanction it, would be construed as illicit trading. The difficult legal situation led a contributor to the Charleston Mercury of Dec. 5, 1859, to consider the advisability of accepting the oath of a negro in court against a white man for trading, provided the slave's master would testify to the truthfulness of the negro offered as a witness.

But with all these precautions the enforcement of the law in the ordinary way seemed near to impossible. It will be explained in a later chapter that there were organized, particularly about 1859, unofficial community associations for the purpose of dealing with the abolitionists and other incendiary persons. But as early as 1850 there had existed similar organizations for dealing with the illicit trader. Indeed it is quite probable that it is these same earlier protective societies against negro trading that were later turned into societies to protect against abolitionism as well, or at least added this to the list of the things they would attend to; or, the disturbed feelings of 1859 gave rise to other organically new societies framed on the same model. But these earlier organizations with vigilance committees were formed to compass the evil of negro trading by lawful prosecution if possible, and by extra-legal methods if necessary. The description of one such organization will suffice as an illustration: At Cartersville (now in Florence county), a small country village, a meeting of the citizens of the community was held, determined to stamp out trafficking with slaves. They appear to have had in mind unlawful means of dealing with the evil, for the first of their resolutions passed was that they would boycott any attorney who would undertake to prosecute their society. They themselves passed resolutions favorable to a heavier punishment for trading to the extent that any person so convicted should be disqualified from giving evidence before a court or of voting or enjoying any of the privileges of citizenship. The Darlington paper remarked editorially on the meeting as follows:

"The proceedings of the Vigilance Society will be read with interest. The negro traders about Cartersville have raised a set of men who will give them trouble. Let us be vigilant, watchful and discreet, determined and unyielding; these rascals can be conquered." A news note in the Keowee Courier (Pickens) of February 19, 1859, has the following:

"Trafficking with Slaves—A number of the citizens of Abbeville District, assembled on the 15th ult. for the purpose of taking measures to prevent illicit traffic between mean white men and the slaves. A vigilance committee was appointed to rid the neighborhood of these pests." These movements, as has just been said, indicate the ineffectiveness of the legal means of dealing with the situation. There was one penalty that had not been tried—that was whipping for the person so offending. In 1850, Governor Seabrook had the following to say of the traffic and its possible remedy:

"Unlawful trading and trafficking with slaves, by which a white person knowingly inflicts upon society, and especially his vicinage, widespread and prolific evils, is perhaps one of the very few offenses deserving of corporal punishment." In 1853 the grand jury of Spartanburg district had noted the growing evil of negro trading and had made the following recommendation, which was repeated in substance in 1857:

"Present as a Nuisance the existing Laws relating to the punishment of Persons convicted for trading with Slaves—that in many cases, perhaps the majority, fine and imprisonment does not operate as a corrective to the evil—and recommend that the law should be so altered as to superadd the punishment of whipping, in such cases as it may be proper in the opinion of the court to inflict." In the spring of 1857 and again at the fall term the Union grand jury, after noting that the law was a dead letter, recommended that the punishment be made corporal. The Williamsburg grand jury in the fall of 1857 recommended that the legislature make whipping the punishment for negro trading. A meeting at Darlington discussed unlawful trafficking and passed resolutions, one of which was a memorial that for the second offense whipping be made the penalty.

The general assembly at its session that winter passed the necessary act, providing that upon a second conviction for negro trading the offender might, unless it happened to be a white woman, in addition to other penalties, receive thirty-nine lashes.

It is not probable that this penalty was ever suffered by many, if it ever occurred at all. None of the sessions journals of the districts examined by the writer records such a sentence. It was probably intended more as a deterrent than as an actual penalty. When this extreme measure was resorted to, it is more probable that it was done by the hands of a mob. The debate in the senate on the measure is enlightening. Senator Tillinghast opposed it in toto. Senator Moses, who seems to have had the bill in charge, stated that there were many requests before the committee which had the bill under consideration from grand juries requesting its passage; he felt that the state had more to fear from the illicit trader than from the abolitionist; "the people have been compelled to organize themselves into vigilance committees and inflict punishment with the lash upon such offenders;" imprisonment had been found to be ineffective; gambling with negroes was common all over the state until whipping was made the penalty for it. Senator Irby approved of the bill, expressing the belief that the threat of corporal punishment would be sufficient to cause them to leave the community rather than submit to it. In the case of gambling only one person to his knowledge had been whipped as punishment.

Another phase of unlawful negro trading was selling or bartering liquor to slaves. There was perhaps much less difficulty encountered in preventing this than in preventing other illicit trading, for under no circumstances is it ordinarily to be presumed that it was agreeable to the master for his slaves to have whiskey. If the master desired it for his own use there was no great difficulty about sending a written order, which was probably done. To keep liquor from the slave was to the interest of everybody except the dealer in such wares; the master's interest was in having a sober laborer, the community's interest was in having an orderly negro in their midst. These interests together perhaps fairly well controlled its sale to the negro in the rural sections. Still, sometimes it was the case that masters gave a small allowance of liquor to the slaves on holiday occasions. Perhaps this custom is referred to in a presentment of the grand jury of Marlborough district in 1849: "We present as a grievance the pernicious practice of allowing negroes the free use of ardent spirits."

The act of 1740 provided a fine of £5 for selling liquor to a slave without a permit. It would seem, however, that until late in the slavery regime the laws on trading were usually resorted to to punish the person who sold liquor to a slave. This further bears out the former statement that the securing of liquor by slaves was not so common. The penalties for trading were adequate and there would be less question as to the circumstances surrounding the deal to interfere with its enforcement. Even after a specific act on selling spirits to slaves was passed probably the case continued to be brought under the charge of unlawful trading, for the penalties were heavier. In none of the dockets to which the writer has had access is there any indictment brought under the specific charge of liquor selling until 1840 or thereabouts. But in 1858 the Court of Appeals decided that a person for one case of selling liquor to a slave could not be convicted for illicit trading and then for selling of liquor to a slave.

In 1831 a law was enacted prohibiting any free negro from owning or operating a still under a penalty of fifty lashes. The wisdom of this as a police precaution is quite evident. No master was allowed under a penalty of a fine of $100 and imprisonment for one month to allow any of his slaves to have any part in the manufacture and sale of alcoholic beverages. In 1850 a white man in Laurens district was found guilty in two cases for "suffering slave to vend spirituous liquors" and fined $50 in each instance. In 1834 an act was passed prohibiting, under a penalty of a fine of $100 and six months' imprisonment, selling liquor to a slave without a permit from his master. Every vendor of alcoholic beverages was to be required before his license was issued to take an oath not to sell to any slave any liquor unless on a permit from his master or overseer, and on application for a renewal of his license he was to be required to take oath that he had not heretofore sold liquor to slaves in violation of law.

As to the enforcement of the laws just referred to some occasional reference will throw light upon the question. In 1744 the Charleston grand jury complained of the habit of selling rum to negroes. In the Columbia Free Press and Hive of September 3, 1831, is an open communication from "Good Order" which for the light it gives is quoted in full:

"To the Honorable Town Council of Columbia:

"As the licenses for the retailing of spirituous liquors will soon expire I take the liberty of respectfully calling your attention to the situation of certain licensed Grog Shops in this town.

"It is a fact public and notorious that many retailers are in the constant habit, day and night and more especially on Sundays, of selling liquor to the negroes, in utter defiance of the laws of the state and of the corporation.

"The Council have the power of putting a stop to practices so disgraceful to the town and ruinous to negro property.

"If the Council will on the first of October next refuse licenses to all those shopkeepers whose houses have been the notorious resort of negroes the evil will be in a great measure remedied. Such a measure will meet the support of every friend of "Good Order."

Here the reader may be cited again to the report of Mayor Robert Y. Hayne, of Charleston, m 1837, quoted in a chapter below, in which he speaks of the effort being made to break up the connection of the colored population with the dram shops. The report of Mayor William Porcher Miles in 1857 is even better and the part relating to this phase is quoted in full:

"When the police was reorganized one of the first objects to which their attention was strenuously directed was the suppression of the practice of selling liquor to slaves and of the illegal traffic with them generally. The extent to which this nefarious business is carried on would surprise and alarm the community were they thoroughly informed on the subject. The number of shops where the negroes habitually meet to drink and gamble, with the proceeds frequently of the robbery of their masters, is very great. The daily confession of the negroes themselves, in the police court, would be sufficient to convince anyone who might entertain a doubt on the subject. Against this great and crying evil the police have waged a constant war. They have thus made themselves odious to a large and (as far as elections go) influential class. And here I deem it my solemn duty to urge upon the citizens of Charleston the necessity of some more efficient legislation for the remedy of abuses which are tending to undermine the institution of slavery in our very midst, year after year, by the moral as well as the physical deterioration of our negroes." A summary of the police court proceedings written daily for the Evening News, of Charleston, in 1856, taken for the month of September as a representative month, shows that nearly all the cases against negroes originate in drunkenness or may in some way be connected with it.

Governor Allston, in 1857, in his annual message deplores the fact that there is so much unlawful selling of liquor to slaves. While he makes this statement there is no reason to believe that it was such a widespread evil or such a systematic disregard of the law as there was in the case of illicit trading with slaves. The law was often doubtless violated, but it was not common or uncontrollable.

86

CHAPTER IX. Slaves Hiring Their Own Time

Up to this point we have considered the slave almost exclusively as an agricultural laborer, living on a large plantation and working under an overseer and driver, or in smaller groups on small farms working perhaps along with the owner and the owner's sons. The system of control for this kind of laborers, all grouped together on small farms with a generous sprinkling of whites or on the larger plantations where whites were fewer, is comparatively simple. But as time went on many of the negroes came to adapt themselves in some measure to their surroundings and to acquire considerable skill as mechanics, blacksmiths, carpenters or similar partially skilled laborers. If the plantation were large the most apt in any line, for instance as carpenter, was likely to be kept at that kind of work on the place all the time. On the smaller farms no such opportunity for developing and making constant use of such special skill was offered. Hence often the owners hired slaves who showed mechanical skill, to other men engaged in that kind of undertaking, because the remuneration for such services per year usually netted a better income than when retained as a "farm hand." Slaves might, of course, be hired to others to work on farms as well. But this was not a permanent arrangement, for the renting out of a slave in this way was not ordinarily profitable, because slaves under over work would rapidly deteriorate and the payment made for them for this purpose was not considerable. But it sometimes occurred as a shift for settling up an estate, where the executor did not wish the farm responsibility, or where the owner had a surplus laborer and disliked to break up the family.

In all these cases the person to whom the slave was hired came to sustain in the eyes of the law the same relation to the slave to protect, care for, and restrain as did the master. The master, of course, always had recourse by law to recover his slave from the custody of the person to whom he was hired in case of cruelty or lack of proper sustentation.

It was not always the case that a slave could be hired to another person except for a long period of time, but he might be able to earn for his master a good income by job work at odd times, realizing more than for being hired to another for a long time. But working out on odd jobs necessarily took him out from under the eye and direct supervision of the master, and nobody else's control was substituted for that of the master. It is easy to see how a slave might be employed in this way exclusively as a source of income to the master so long as he proved faithful, industrious and orderly. This privilege would afford him quite a good deal more of freedom than the field hand had. It may here be remarked that the place of a field hand was regarded by the slave as the most menial, so much so that a threat to a house servant that he would be transferred to the field was usually quite sufficient to make him more diligent and attentive to his duties. Thus it often came about that in many cases the master had a complete arrangement or agreement with his slave that the latter would be allowed to work at his trade, or job work, going and coming as he pleased provided he brought the master each week or month a specified sum or part of his earnings, all over and above that amount being allowed to the slave. This was called the slave's "hiring out his time," or more accurately it was the master "hiring out" the slave's time to the slave himself for which the slave paid a stipulated amount. The custom of "hiring out" the slave's time was not common in the rural districts. At any rate it was not so common as in the cities and smaller towns, where it came to be really the established economic order of things. Indeed, in the cities where a slaveowner kept slaves with him on his premises his relation to the public was not unlike the liveryman. The advantage to the master was that the slave needed less constant care than the horse. This statement, however, is not to be taken to imply that there was a distinct class considerable in numbers who thus, so to speak, capitalized their slaves. The slavery system was based essentially on the agricultural regime and no other. Its system of control was fixed on the basis of the slave's forever remaining a "field hand" or at best remaining attached to a plantation. But the city had other work for the slave to do which rendered the original plan of regulation cumbersome and unsuitable. The gradual advance of the negroes in acquiring skill was slowly solving the problem of emancipation. It would seem that this hiring out of the slave would have proven to be the point of departure from the old slavery system to a new economic organization of labor; not that the movement would have been rapid in South Carolina, much more conservatism being felt here than in most other slaveholding communities.

Legal emancipation except by special enactment was forbidden after 1820. But the hiring of their own time to slaves was often used to bring about virtually the same result. It sometimes was the reward of faithfulness or the way of showing unusual interest in any particular slave. Here opens a field of conjecture: How soon would an industrial emancipation of the fittest have been accomplished by this quasi-freedom? Would it have ever reached the negroes on the plantation? There is very serious doubt whether slaves allowed during the greater part of their lifetime to hire their own time were ever afterwards held as slaves by heirs of the estate.

But this system of hiring slaves their time involved certain difficulties. It made the slaves so favored practically free from control and gave opportunities for becoming disorderly in the community. Indeed, it sometimes encouraged their becoming idle and indulged their indolence, and in order to meet the weekly payments to their masters, the price of their quasi-freedom, they had an unfortunate inducement to steal. A communication to the Charleston Courier of September 12, 1850, complained that no domestic servants could be had because the slaves were allowed to hire their time and then complain to their master at the end of the month that they could secure no work to do. The grand jury of Union district had the following to say in the spring of 1857 of the custom of hiring to negroes their time:

"Certain individuals are in the habit of hiring out to their slave his own time which he spends in trafficking about over the country very much to the loss of the farmer who finds it difficult to supply his own table with eggs and poultry. Everything is picked up by these negro pedlars and as there is a sort of free masonry about negro intercourse it is hard to detect the wrongdoer."

To the same effect is a quotation from an editorial in the Rising Sun (Newberry) of May 19, 1858, that gives the worst possible view of the custom; very probably the picture is much overdrawn:

"We believe now, always have believed and always will believe while we can kick, that the plan of hiring slaves their own time is unwise, impolitic and works injury to the hired as well as to the other slaves whereever they are thrown. It renders slaves dissatisfied, makes them worthless and lazy, corrupts and spoils them, and all others with whom they associate. They become liars, rogues, villains and perpetrate anything that will enable them free of work to pay their wages. We have our eyes on one or two slaves who hire their own time, rent houses and pretend to do, nobody knows what. It is objectionable and ought to be done away with."'

It will be seen that this practice acted as a virtual suspension of all slave regulation and if widely established would have led to great evils. Hence from 1712 there were laws prohibiting it. The codes of 1712 and 1740 prohibited it with small fines. An act of 1822 made any slave who had been permitted to "hire out" his time liable to seizure, confiscation and sale as in case of a slave illegally introduced into the state. The act of 1849 made more intelligent provision by making the penalty merely a fine of $50 on the owner of the slave allowed to hire his time, one-half going to the informer.

Abundant evidence can be cited to show that the law was almost totally disregarded and that apparently no effort was made to enforce it. A city ordinance of Charleston of 1800 (recognizing apparently that the law was being constantly violated) undertook to regulate the practice by requiring every owner who had slaves hired out on their own account to secure a badge from the city authorities on payment of a small fee. This was put in more systematic form in 1846 by a provision that the badge should show in what kind of work the slave was engaged and date (year issued) and that it must be worn by the slave in a conspicuous place; failure by the master to comply was punishable with a fine of two dollars. An editorial in the Charleston Mercury of December 10, 1859, says that few even of these badges were worn, but that it was understood that the police had been ordered to enforce the law. An ordinance of the town of Marion in 1858 was similar although it appears to have been primarily a revenue measure. It prohibited any owner to allow his slave "to follow any permanent employment" except after paying a small license fee.

Of the class of negroes to which this custom gave rise Pollard says:

"You must know that our colored gentry (many of whom, as the custom is here, make considerable money by hiring their own time and paying their masters a stated sum for the privilege) not only maintain parsons and build churches, but hire carriages to attend them." The grand juries of Charleston as early as 1734 had complained of the evils of the practice.

The grand jury of Darlington in 1849 said:

"We present the practice of negroes hiring their own time from their owners and owning horses and travelling in buggies, wagons, etc., as a nuisance in this district calculated to produce a spirit of insubordination amongst the slave population." The Newberry grand jury in 1859 said:

"The law in relation to slaves hiring their own time is not enforced with sufficient promptness and efficiency as to accomplish the object designed by its enactment."

No effort appears to have been made to enforce the law. The available court records of nine counties reveal only two cases of prosecutions for this offense; one case was in Darlington district in 1855 in which the document was returned by the grand jury "no bill." The other was in Marlborough in the same year, the bill bearing the following returns: "true bill," "not arrested," "not guilty."

Industrial competition finally showed its hand. The skilled free negro workmen were formidable enough, but to these was added this semi-free class of slaves. The Vesey plot of 1822 had called attention to the danger from this growing class of colored laborers. In a series of articles published in the South Carolina State Gazette in October and November of that year, and later printed in pamphlet form, said of the skilled negro laborer in connection with the problem of his control:

"The great fundamental principle should be that the slave should be kept as much confined as possible to agricultural labors. These so employed are found to be the most orderly and obedient of the slaves, ... There should be no black mechanics or artisans, at least in the cities. These are placed, by the nature of their employments, much more from under the eye and inspection of their masters, and they acquire vicious habits injurious to themselves as well as their owners, and of evil example to other slaves." It appears also that the organizations of mechanics had in three different memorials already petitioned the legislature for relief from competition with slaves who were allowed to hire their time and work out as mechanics. These together with a recent presentment of the Charleston grand jury and proposed bills to remedy the evils complained of were referred to a legislative committee, whose report reviewed the acts of 1822 and 1849 on the subject and certain proposed bills, expressing the opinion that the latter cover the same ground already covered by the laws previously enacted. The committee found itself very much at loss for a remedy but suggested that certain laborers from among the slaves be allowed to hire their time. No law came as a result of their suggestions. Some of their statements on the subject are well worth quoting: "The evil complained of is, that slaves are allowed to go at large, exercise all the privileges of free persons, make contracts, do work, and every way live and conduct themselves as if they were not slaves. . . . The evil is, he buys the control of his own time from his owner. By the payment of a stipulated amount of wages he avoids the discipline and surveillance of his master and is separated from his observation and superintendence. We agree fully with the Memorialists who complain of this evil—but the ground is much more general than the one set up in these Bills. The evil lies in the breaking down the relation between master and slave—the removal of the slave from the master's discipline and control and the assumption of freedom and independence on the part of the slave, the idleness, disorder and crime which are consequential, and the necessity thereby created for additional police regulations to keep them in subjection and order, and the trouble and expense they involve.

"Yet there is something to be said in relation to carrying that relation into effect. We are a slaveholding people habituated to slave labor and domestic labor of our state. We have towns and villages, however, where ordinary labor is to be performed which can be done either by whites or negroes. We are accustomed to black labor and it would create a revolution to drive it away. The domestic servants, most of the common laborers and porters, draymen, wagoners and cartmen and on the seaboard stevedores are mostly negroes; but they are all included in the general inhibition of the acts of 1822 and 1849. It would be impossible to have this sort of slave labor, if there must be a contract with the owner for every specific job—as for instance the transportation of a load in a wagon or dray, the carrying of a passenger's trunk to or from a railroad, etc. The subject is, therefore, full of difficulty and until you can change the direction of the public prejudice, prepossession and habit you can never enforce a law that conflicts with them."

94

CHAPTER X. The Slave Trade, Foreign and Domestic

The foreign slave trade though not coming properly within the range of our subject may be referred to at this point. In 1787 an act was passed prohibiting the trade entirely, both foreign and domestic. The acts were temporary but were renewed from time to time before their expiration until 1803. Provision was made, however, to allow persons who intended to become bona fide citizens to bring their slaves into the state with them, or any slaves acquired by a marriage formed without the state could also be introduced. Every precaution was thrown around the act and heavy penalties for its violation were provided. Notwithstanding the vigilance of the officers of the law, Governor James B. Richardson, in his annual message of 1803, said that the traffic had continued and apparently could not be stopped. The message betrays the trace of a desire that the restrictions be removed, and in the same year the legislature repealed all former acts prohibiting the traffic, while the repealing measure still prohibited the importance of any male slave over fifteen years of age from any sister state. The breaking of a New Orleans levee would perhaps be the best illustration of the inundation of blacks that flooded the state. It was worse because this was the only state which opened its ports to them at this time. During the four years that the foreign trade was allowed until 1808, when the traffic was forbidden by federal statute, 39,075 slaves were thrown into the state.

One of the disastrous effects of the passage of the law, though small comparatively if we are to believe Ramsay, was to cause more than a hundred Quakers, a thrifty, lawabiding class of citizens, who had religious scruples about slavery, to leave the state for Ohio, selling their lands at a sacrifice. During the first two decades of the nineteenth century about twelve hundred Quakers left South Carolina for the middle West as the result probably of the laws of this period favorable to the slavery interests. Whole communities left Piney Grove in Marlborough district and Bush River in Newberry district.

Efforts were made to repeal the wide-open policy of the act of 1803, pleas being made by the governor in 1805 and again in 1806 on every available consideration. One was that the state should take action before it was forced upon her by congress, as was likely to be the case by 1808. But the appeals were futile. In 1805 the lower house passed a bill prohibiting the traffic, but it was lost on second reading in the senate by a vote of 15 to 16 because the upper house insisted that the interstate traffic be permitted if the foreign were prohibited. In 1806 a similar bill passed the house of representatives with only two dissenting votes but failed on second reading in the senate by a vote of 16 to 16. Perhaps the interests of the slave trade could not be overcome and the state possibly hoped to gain some advantage from the slaves entering at Charleston and Georgetown with a view to being then sent west.

The agitation for the reopening of the slave trade in the fifties may be passed over briefly. Dubois finds the desire for cheap labor at the bottom of this agitation, and this certainly must have been a contributing cause. But the general controversy over the slavery question must have had another reason, which begot a sort of dare-devil spirit on the part of Southern blood to show its confidence in the righteousness of their cause, to overcome any doubts that were arising in their minds. The majority of Southern sentiment would not, it can be safely said, have tolerated the suggestion but for the offset it afforded abolitionism. The fuse was fired by the capture of the Echo, an African slave vessel, near Charleston harbor in August, 1858, with three hundred and six slaves aboard—afterwards reshipped to Africa by the Colonization Society. The legislature in 1857 appointed a committee to investigate the desirability of reopening the foreign trade, referring to it the recommendation of the governor to that effect. The majority of the committee—all but one—reported favorably to the project! This leads up to the question of the interstate traffic, which has a closer bearing on the question of police control. It is true that had there been a continued influx of the foreign element it would have to be studied more fully in its bearing on the conduct of the negroes already present within the state but as it soon ceased we turned to the domestic trade. The argument offered for prohibiting the introduction of slaves from other states was to prevent the speculator from loading up the community with undesirable slaves. As was the case in the latter half century of the existence of American slavery the slave was much more valuable on the rice and cotton plantation of Carolina than he was in Virginia. There would be a tendency then in the absence of any restrictions for the state to increase its slave population in a way second only in evil to that of foreign importation.

But a more important reason is that referred to, that the professional speculators who would have the opportunity to go through the state buying up cheaply the unruly, dangerous, lazy slaves and to unload them at a good price in another. Here was a Pandora's box of trouble for the community, and a source of dread for the state. The grand jury of Spartanburg district, bordering on the state of North Carolina, had the following to say of the interstate traffic in the fall of 1816:

"We present as a serious and most lamentable grievance the bringing in of slaves from other parts of the Union: the practice is an imposition on our citizens and dangerous to the safety of the State; we do trust that our Legislature will, without delay, take the case under their consideration."

It is stated in its worst light in the message of Governor D. R. Williams in 1816. He said in part:

"It is not possible that your deliberations on these subjects can be concluded before that remorseless, merciless traffic, which brings among us slaves of all descriptions from other states, which is a reproach to our morals and an outrage to our feelings, shall press on you for correction. It is time the course of ceaseless cupidity, alike regardless of country and consequences, should be arrested, high time that our streets and highways should be freed from the crowds of suffering victims that are constantly dragged through them to minister to insatiable avarice. The lights of humanity, a wise policy, the prayers of the just, all require that the delightful avocations of domestic life should be no longer defiled by the presence of convicts and malefactors."

The act of 1816, to prevent the introduction of slaves from sister states for sale, was very drastic in its provisions. It provided that slaves unlawfully introduced might be seized and sold, one-half the proceeds going to the informer; the trader was to be fined $50 for each slave sold and for a second series of offenses to be declared guilty of a felony; any person buying such slaves knowing them to be illegally introduced into the state was to be fined $400; the tax collector was authorized to require every slaveowner to make oath that he had not purchased any slave contrary to the law. But the law was not observed. The difficulty lay in the method of its enforcement. Governor Pickens, in his message of 1818, said:

"It is believed that this law, which is thought so repugnant to the interests of many of our fellow citizens, is violated in many instances with impunity; as no one will incur the odium attached to the character of an informer."

Another difficulty was the exceptions that many desired to have made to the law by special act to permit the importation of certain slaves. The legislative news letter to the (Charleston) City Gazette, printed on December 4, 1817, has this utterance as to the number of petitions:

"The number already petitioned for amount to 735 and God knows how many more will be presented before the end of the session."

In view of the frequent violations of the law Governor Pickens submitted to the wisdom of the legislators in his message of 1818 the question whether or not the act of 1816 should be repealed. The act rescinding the former law was passed. The private correspondence to the Charleston Courier of Dec. 12, 1818, describes the debate in the lower house as "one of the most eloquent and animated that has taken place on that floor for many years."

The seamen act of 1835 has two sections limiting the bringing in of slaves as servants from the outside, if they had been north of the Potomac or in the West Indies or other points to the south of Carolina. This act was amended in 1847 so as to permit slaves to be introduced from Cuba. With these exceptions it seems that after 1818 the bars were let down to permit unrestricted trade. Thus it will be seen that South Carolina assumed for the benefit of the large planters the responsibility for making the state an open market for the surplus slaves of other states.

CHAPTER XI. Stealing and Harboring of Slaves and Kidnapping of Free Negroes

The recognition of the interests of the slaveholder cannot be better illustrated than by the rigorous enforcement of the severe penalty for stealing and carrying away slaves, often called "inveigling," which deprived the master of his property. It was regarded as one of the most heinous crimes that could be committed, even worse apparently than the murder of a slave.

But neither the interest of the master nor the desire to protect the comfort of the slave was the only reason why the penalty was severe and the law rigorously enforced. Slave-stealing was dangerous in that it threatened the entire stability of the whole system and was subversive of the interests of society. The slave-stealer was the anarchist of Southern serfdom. Suppose it had been allowed to become a common offense: property in slaves would have been insecure; other property would have been endangered by the lawlessness of the depredators; lives of the whites would not have been secure, for it would have encouraged and made possible insurrection and general disorder which was the nightmare of the Southern white; the slave thief would have been in position, with the assistance of his captives, to carry out his plans of the highwayman with organized method.

Add to this the ineffectiveness of any penalty short of execution and it will be clear how capital punishment came to be regarded as the proper one. A fine could have been recouped by another steal or two when a "likely" negro was worth $1,000, even if we suppose that he parted with his stolen property at half price. A prison sentence which sometimes may have been imposed in lieu of the death penalty frequently ended in an escape, owing to the desperate character of the thieves and also to the fact that several of them often acted together and gave each other assistance to escape. However, it was not until

1754 that slave stealing had become sufficiently prevalent to demand enactment of the highest penalty.

But the danger becomes more formidable when, as it appears there were, though rarely perhaps, organized bands of outlaws, who like highway robbers of earlier days, made this their means of earning a livelihood. The most notorious of these bands was one which was led by Murrel in the thirties and early forties and was brought to bay by the Tennessee authorities. A news item in the Charleston Courier of September 9, 1846, mentions the capture of a young white man at Cheraw who was suspected by his display of money of having assisted in the escape of four negroes from the community. When arrested he implicated another white man and a negro, the latter of whom was caught at Raleigh, North Carolina, and duly executed. The white man was thought to be one of the original Murrel gang. The method used, as appears from the more or less embellished story of Murrel in the disclosure to Stewart, was to approach a slave while at work; the slave, who perhaps betrayed a longing desire for some kind of change, was asked how he liked his master; if he showed an ill feeling toward his master he was invited to escape usually at night on a signal to a given rendezvous. The slave's co-operation was secured by imposing upon his credulity with the story that he was being transported by a friend to a free state or at least that he would be placed in more favorable surroundings than he enjoyed at present. The negro, often easily deceived, did as was directed. After a sufficient distance had been reached—Arkansas was a favorite place for the Murrel gang—the slave was sold. The new master was likely to be no improvement over the former and the thief, who appeared to be a sort of savior in need to the now adventurous black, turned up again and, with the negro's assistance, the stolen black is whisked away to another distance and resold.

These highwaymen were shifty enough to understand that an advertisement for a runaway slave gave to any white person the right to arrest and return such slave to his master or overseer as a captured runaway. Naturally the master or overseer, when he found that the slave was gone, advertised for him thinking most likely he had run away, as this was more or less common. Hence on being caught the thief could plead that it was in an effort to return the runaway that he was found in the slave's company. It will be remembered that the slave was not competent to give evidence as to what had happened. Even if he "talked" it could be used only as a clue; it is hardly probable that the slave, who was conscious of the effect upon the master of his own co-operation to cheat the master out of his services, could or would give a coherent account of what had passed since he was aware that it was not likely to better his case if a sound whipping was in store for him.

We may here inquire as to the frequency of the crime of slave stealing and its punishment. The Charleston Courier of June 2, 1809, in a news item tells of the pardon of two persons convicted of slave stealing. Governor Drayton, in his annual message to the general assembly in November of the same year, mentioned the fact that there had been five convictions with the death penalty in each case for this crime during the year then coming to a close and that one prisoner was awaiting trial in Charleston at the time. He defended his record for pardons of slave stealers by referring to popular sentiment, a considerable part of which was against so severe a penalty. He then proceeded to shift the responsibility for the criticism of the severity of the penalty upon the legislature by saying that it they did not see fit to change the law he desired to serve notice that there would hereafter be no executive interference with sentences of death imposed by the courts for this offense. No change was made in the penalty by law. Accordingly, in a proclamation of a reward of $200 by the governor in the following March for an overseer who had left a farm on the Waccamaw carrying some slaves with him, he added:

"And I do hereby earnestly require and strictly enjoin all officers of this state, civil and military, and all authorities of the same to be vigilant in arresting, trying and bringing to justice and to due and lawful punishment all persons charged with negro stealing; which has of late increased to a degree, requiring such punishment as the laws of the state authorize; and which shall in proper cases be carried into full effect, so far as depends upon the authorities and powers with which I am invested." That the authorities were in earnest and that this policy of carrying the law into effect was continued appears from two instances.

In a news item in The Times (Charleston) of February 25, 1813, is the notice of an execution at Barnwell for "horse and negro stealing"; the item reads:

"He was strongly guarded by the militia, both foot and horse, as it was rumored a rescue would be attempted, the sentence by many, being thought too severe—executive clemency having been strenuously withheld notwithstanding repeated strong applications in his favor." The other instance is the resolution of the Charleston City Council of June 17, 1816, providing for the purchase of space in the Charleston Courier for a month's publication in each issue of the act to prevent slave stealing. This was done apparently with a view to prevent anybody's acting through ignorance of the serious consequences.

Instances of executions for slave stealing could be multiplied. Chapman, in the Annals of Newberry, makes mention of the escape from the Newberry jail of a white man charged with negro stealing, his capture, trial, conviction and commutation of the death sentence after he had been taken to the scaffold. Or, of another at Darlington in 1846 who paid the penalty. But one of the most notorious cases occurred in Sumter district, where three slaves were stolen from Willie Spain. The thief was caught and a true bill was found against him at the April term of court in 1838. After an unsuccessful effort to escape he finally succeeded in "breaking jail" on July 30, 1838. An unusually long "presentment" of the sheriff by the grand jury followed at the next term of court with a very vigorous criticism of that officer on account of the escape. The sheriff was ordered to "show cause" for nonperformance of duty, which he did presumably with satisfaction for no fine or other penalty was imposed on the sheriff in so far as the records show. The criminal was not finally arraigned until 1844 when he was convicted and sentenced to be hanged. All of the papers in the clerk of court's office in the case are preserved, and it is probable that due care was observed for the safekeeping of the prisoner, who it may be inferred was at last executed since nothing to the contrary appears.

An interesting case of slave stealing which affected South Carolina occurred in Virginia in 1839. It serves to show the attitude of the South toward the North when sometimes slaves were assisted to escape or stolen outright. Three negro sailors aided a slave to escape to New York. Requisition for the return of the offenders who were regarded as fugitives from justice was made upon the governor of New York, by the Governor of Virginia. The requisition was dishonored, though the escaped slave was recovered, on the ground that slave stealing as a crime had no legal existence in the state of New York. This sounded the alarm to the South. South Carolina passed a rigid inspection act in 1841 against all vessels clearing for New York—the inspector's fee being $10 to be collected from the ship owner—to make sure that no slaves were being concealed on board and were being carried away. The captain of such vessel was also to enter into bond of $1,000 to guarantee the pay for the loss of any slave he might be carrying away clandestinely; he was also required to take oath to the same effect. The governor was given the power to suspend the operation of this act discriminating against New York provided he were officially informed that the requisition of the governor of Virginia for the return of the fugitives had been complied with. Meantime the New York legislature had passed another still more stringent act to prevent the return of runaways, providing a fine of $500 under the charge of kidnapping to carry away any former slave from the state without a hearing. To secure a hearing the person must enter into a bond of $1,000 given by a citizen of the state of New York to secure the costs. In 1842 the South Carolina legislature passed an act supplementary to the one of 1841. It seems, however, that South Carolina had to suffer from its own policy, for the inspection which appears to have been well enforced worked a hardship on trade within the state. Merchants of Charleston and Georgetown complained of the hindrance to business which it caused. But the only action taken on their petitions to the legislature was to refer them to a committee. The committee's report shows that the fees annually collected until 1847 amounted to $1,500, but for the first eleven months of 1847 they had run up to $1,890.

Closely akin to the stealing of slaves was the "harboring" of slaves. The presumption in harboring seems to have been that it was an effort to deprive the master temporarily of the services of his slave. Then harboring was somewhat like assisting him to run away or becoming an accessory before the fact of slave stealing. In some instances the motive may have been to aid a slave who was thought to have been abused by his master. Harboring under the act of 1821 was punishable with a maximum fine of $1,000 and imprisonment at the discretion of the court; or the person injured could bring a civil action for damages.

The Sumter county records show three convictions in 1827 for harboring, one person so charged being sentenced to four months' imprisonment and the other two to a fine of $1,000 and one year's imprisonment each. Five other persons similarly charged whose names appear on the records are found "not guilty," "no bill," or were discharged. The available Darlington criminal records show nine indictments for harboring, some of which reach the "true bill" stage, but only one is recorded as having been convicted and in this case no penalty is attached. The Williamsburg county records show only one such case, and the defendant was acquitted. The Newberry county "index" shows four such bills entered, two of which were returned after trial "guilty." The other two were returned "no bill" by the grand jury. Kershaw district has only one recorded instance and the person charged is found guilty but no sentence appears. Marlborough district has only two recorded cases, one of which was nolle pressed and the other was returned "no bill." Two cases only were brought in Laurens and both were "struck off." Union district had six cases of harboring, in only two of which convictions were secured, though no sentence appears. In Greenville district six cases are on record, in only two of which convictions are reached. One case was against a white man and woman, the sentence being a fine of $5 and one month's imprisonment. In another the penalty was $200 and six months' imprisonment. Spartanburg also records an even six cases, in only one of which conviction was reached, the sentence being one month's imprisonment.

It sometimes happened also that free negroes fell into the hands of these robbers and were carried some distance and sold as slaves. Whatever other disadvantages free negroes labored under, the community would look upon this as a most pernicious evil although the self-interest of the slaveowner was not present to protect him. Most of the slave laws were based primarily upon the pecuniary interest of the slaveowner. Apparently there was no law against the abduction of free negroes until 1837. The law passed in that year provided for a fine of $1,000 and twelve months' imprisonment as a minimum penalty for any person assisting in such an abduction; if the theft succeeded the offender was to receive an additional punishment of thirty-nine lashes. The penalty was light in comparison with that for stealing a slave—as no white person's property interest was at stake. Per se stealing a free negro child, by which act it was deprived of freedom and reduced to slavery, would seem far more reprehensible than carrying off a slave, by which the latter was merely transferred from one owner to another even though the new master was not so humane as the former.

Collins, in his monograph on the Domestic Slave Trade, gives it as his opinion that this kidnapping of free negroes, especially children, was frequent. The lateness of acts which prohibited it appearing on the statute books cannot be taken as evidence that the cases were rare. For the moral sense of the community does not appear to have been especially acute on this subject, as we shall see later that there was a serious agitation that all free negroes should be enslaved. Still it is true that unless the free negro's guardian or some white person interested himself in the case, the colored freeman was left legally and practically without protection. Just how frequently such kidnappings occurred it would be difficult to say. The court records of course cannot be taken as a final estimate for in the records of the county clerk of court's offices examined by the writer only one such case occurs, namely, in Darlington district in 1846—and it was "struck off." As evidence that kidnapping had been common before the law of 1837 was passed may be mentioned the following scheme of unscrupulous persons for reducing to slavery and selling free negroes which is referred to by the grand jury of Charleston in 1816:

"We present as a grievance the show of lawful proceedings, which has been fictitiously given by some persons to the horrible practice of inducing free negroes in jail or in debt to bind themselves for a trifling sum for several years, and by a transfer in the indenture and a chain of inhuman proceedings cause them to be sold into the interior or out of the state, by which means they may be deprived of their freedom." In the Columbia Free Press and Hive of April 9, 1831, the case of such kidnapping of a free negro child is mentioned in a news item, and inquiry for information as to it is made though the theft occurred across the line in North Carolina at Chapel Hill. Another instance is mentioned in the Reports of the Court of Appeals of 1841 of a free negro who had been brought from Florida and confined in the work-house at

Charleston for sale. He communicated the facts of his freedom and the name and address of his guardian to the warden, who became sufficiently interested to investigate and found the statement true. The captor doubtless meantime having had his suspicions aroused, had decided that the atmosphere of that community was unwholesome.

CHAPTER XII. Runaway Slaves

If one glances through a Southern newspaper published before 1860 the first thing that the eye is likely to fall upon will be an advertisement of some ten lines or more at the left-hand corner of which there is a rude cut of a negro in flight, carrying in one hand or thrown over his back on a stick a bag representing food for a few days. At the top of the notice in bold face type are the words: $10 reward; sometimes $50 or even $100. The following is a good specimen taken at random from the Southern Times and State Gazette of July 10, 1835:

"TEN DOLLARS REWARD Will be paid for the apprehension and confinement in any jail in this state of a negro man, named Dublin, who absconded from the plantation of Dr. , in Lexington district on the 30th of June.

"Said Dublin is about fortyfive years of age, five feet four inches high, spare made, with his under jaw apparently too long for the upper one. He has a very dark complexion and speaks somewhat broken as he is an African by birth."

The number of notices appearing in any issue varies from only two or three to a score. The early Charleston papers of the eighteenth century often have column after column of them, showing that escapes were common in the earlier times; while the Abbeville papers of the forties and fifties have almost none.

Among these notices of runaways are other advertisements of captures, though they are fewer, for often when captured if the owner were known the slave was returned directly. Some enterprising newspapers used a small cut representing a negro humbled by capture with his hands clasped almost between his knees and the hand of a burly white man resting on his shoulder. This cut was to distinguish the notice of a capture from that of a runaway.

The following from the Camden Journal of January 6, 1827, is typical:

"COMMITTED

"To Lancaster jail a negro man who calls his name Jack, of a dark complexion, about five feet eight or ten inches high (marked with the whip upon his back), about fifty years of age: says that he belongs to Capt., of Oglethorpe county, Georgia. The owner is requested to prove property, pay charges and take him away. S. L. D."

A whipping for laziness or misconduct, or merely the fear of a whipping, was often sufficient to cause a slave "to take to the woods." The master's treatment and the slave's temperament were the factors determining the possibility and frequency of a slave's running away. Slaves were, it is quite true, sometimes persuaded by unscrupulous whites or free negroes or other runaways "to run." But when the conditions by which the slaves were surrounded were good and the plantation discipline firm though humane, and the slave not of a roving disposition, outside influences were rarely effective. There were others of a nervous or a dare-devil disposition who on slightest provocation prayed "Lord, foot help body," and were not seen any more for days or months, and sometimes never again. A master who was weakly lenient—there were few—was, so to speak, held up by a threat implied in the slave's demeanor that he would run away. These chronic runaways were often "sold running" or "sold in the woods," which means that while the negro was away on an escapade the master transferred his title to the slave to another at a very much reduced price, the purchaser taking the chances of recovering the fugitive. A slaveowner gave notice in the South Carolina Gazette of June 28, 1835, that some of his negroes "are constantly running away" and offered a standing reward for the capture and return of these at any time.

One may ask what the purpose of the slave was in running away; did he have any objective point to reach, or was it merely an aimless temporary escape? It was often both. Sometimes he would leave home temporarily for only a few days, and soon hunger, exposure and loneliness would drive him back to the master's quarters. A whipping often awaited him, but if he returned of his own accord and it was not the repetition of a similar former offense, in order to encourage his further faithfulness, a wise master dealt leniently with him. If he was captured and returned he usually received a severe whipping.

The mention of the captor calls for some account of the laws dealing with runaways. The provisions of the law of 1712 on the subject reveals the most striking stupidity perhaps to be found in slave legislation. Graded tortures for the runaway varying in severity from slitting the nose to cutting off one foot were provided for a first, a second and further repetition of the offense. It was made the duty of the master by law to inflict such punishments. But there is but little reason for believing that any such except the milder were ever inflicted as punishments; for if such mutilation did not positively injure the slave so as to make him less useful as a servant, it would at least become a sign of his running proclivities in case he was ever offered for sale. These mutilations, though abolished or superseded by the act of 1740, were sometimes held up by the patrol as a terror to the slave; and there is related in a decision of the Constitutional Court, in a suit over a slave in 1823 as a part of the facts, that the slave had had his ears cropped for burglary. About the only provision of the act of 1740 and of subsequent acts relating to runaways made it the duty of any person capturing a runaway slave to return him to the master immediately or to turn him over to the sheriff within four days. It was not lawful for the captor to retain a runaway slave in his custody, for this would naturally give him opportunity secretly to use the slave's services until the master should find him. The sheriff upon receiving a runaway gave notice in the newspapers. The owner upon claiming the slave was required to pay the necessary expenses of his capture and confinement. If the slave should be unclaimed after eighteen months he was to be sold at public outcry, to defray the expenses of his keep, or "poundage" as it was sometimes called, any balance over expenses to go into the public funds.

There were in some communities persons who made it their business to hunt runaway slaves for their owners for a fee. The Rising Sun, of Newberry, on July 28, 1858, carried an advertisement placed by two men who promised that at any time they would respond to a call for their services for $5 per diem "whether successful or not." "All captures $10 without resistance, where there is resistance, $10 to $50; have dogs and are always ready to attend to business." The autobiography of Stroyer, a negro, says his master kept a man on the plantation to hunt runaway negroes with dogs.

Often, particularly in the lower part of the state, several runaway slaves would band together and form a sort of runaway camp in the swamps where they lived in hiding, maintaining themselves by theft from the neighboring fields and fowl houses. They carried with them rude utensils with which they cooked their meals over the fire.

The following news item from the Marion Star of June 18, 1861, will give a fair picture of such a camp:

"Runaways—Last Tuesday a party of gentlemen from this place went in search of runaways who were thought to be in a swamp two miles from here. A trail was discovered which, winding about much, conducted the party to a knoll in the swamp on which corn, squashes, and peas were growing and a camp had been burnt. Continuing the search, another patch of corn, etc., was found and a camp from which several negroes fled, leaving two small negro children, each about a year old. . . . There were several guns fired at the negroes who fled from the camp but none proved effectual. The camp seemed well provided with meal, cooking utensils, blankets, etc. The party returned, having taken the two children, twelve guns and one axe. . . . Means should immediately be taken for the capture of these runaways, as they are probably lurking about this place." One such gang of outlaws was serious enough in 1816 to cause the governor to order a special foray by the militia. He gives the following account of it in his message to the legislature in that year:

"A few runaway negroes, concealing themselves in the swamps and marshes contiguous to Combahee and Ashepoo rivers, not having been interrupted in their petty plunderings for a long time, formed the nucleus around which the ill-disposed and audacious near them gathered until at length their robberies became too serious to be suffered with impunity. Attempts were then made to disperse them, which, either from insufficiency of numbers or bad arrangement, served by their failure only to encourage a wanton destruction of property. Their force now became alarming, not less from its numbers than from the arms and amunition with which it was supplied. The peculiar situation of that part of our coast rendered access to them difficult, while the numerous creeks and water courses through the marshes and around the islands furnished them easy opportunities in plunder, not only the planters in open day, but the inland coasting trade also, without leaving a trace of their movements by which they could be pursued. There was but one more stage to a state of things altogether intolerable, to prevent which I felt it my duty to use the public force and public money. I, therefore, ordered Col. Wm. Youngblood to take the necessary measures for suppressing them, and authorized him to incur the necessary expenses of such an expedition. This was immediately executed. By a judicious employment of the militia under his command he either captured or destroyed the whole body."

This will show that the runaway was a menace to the peace of the community and affected not only the master but other persons who might be the victims of his depredation. It was with that feeling that more than a hundred years earlier the following resolution was passed by the colonial assembly:

"The House being informed that there are several negroes run away from their masters, and keep out, armed, and robbing and plundering houses and plantations, and putting the inhabitants of this Province in great fear and terror. Resolved by this House that the Governor be addressed to take effectual care to apprehend, take and suppress the said runaways and assure his Honor that this House will, at all times, be ready to concur with the Governor and Council in defraying the expenses of soe good and necessary a designe."

With a similar feeling the Charleston grand jury, in its presentment in 1776, recommended, "that all fugitives after so many months' absence should be deemed outlaws, and subject to death without sentence or expense to the province."

The following quotation from the Senate Journal of Dec. 6, 1816, will illustrate that at a later date the runaway was regarded and treated very much as an outlaw:

"The report on the petition of Edward Brailsford, praying compensation for the loss of two runaway negroe slaves who were killed by a patrole, viz: That they have had the same under consideration and are of the opinion that the prayer thereof ought not to be granted, the more especially as there is no provision made by law for the payment of such losses." Another evil from which the South suffered was the enticing away by abolitionists through the "underground railroad." South Carolina suffered less in this respect than the border states. Conditions similar, however, in their effects to this were when the settlement in Florida, which until 1819 was Spanish, continued to seduce the Carolina slaves from their loyalty. It is mentioned here, for while probably only a comparatively few were lost to the state in that way, still it was a problem in which the Southern slaveowner was interested. Not only was the abolitionist interested but the slave thief had greater opportunity to ply his business. DeBow's Review estimated that the South lost 1,540 slaves every year in this way. The Rising Sun (Newberry) on January 18, 1860, quoted another authority to the effect that there were probably 45,000 slaves in Canada at that time. Siebert estimates that between 1830 and 1860 Ohio aided in the escape of "not less than" 40,000 slaves, more than one thousand per annum; and that during the last quarter century of the existence of slavery in the South Philadelphia aided in 9,000 escapes.

CHAPTER XIII. The Seamen Acts

There was, as has just been intimated, a constant distrust of the negroes and particularly any decided increase of the free negro population by immigration. This was not without reason, for a free negro could easily enter from the outside and conduct insurrectionary movements as was actually the case in the Vesey plot.

The people of the state and the authorities found it comparatively easy to deal with the casual free negro immigrant. But after the disclosure of the Vesey plot it was deemed unsafe to allow the temporary presence of free negroes who might happen to be in the crews of trading vessels. Their fears were founded on altogether possible conditions; such a colored seaman might distribute incendiary literature or by the air of superiority to which the race is prone cause dissatisfaction among the slave population. But the means for preventing this undesirable contact was not the happiest of expedients—it was drastic to say the least, though it was the method of other states as well as South Carolina. This law of 1822 was none other than an order to the sheriff to arrest and closely confine any free negroes who happened to be in the crew of any trading vessel coming into port and retain them in custody until the vessel was ready to leave. The captain was held responsible under heavy penalties for the due removal of such negroes when the vessel should leave, and was held also financially liable for the jail fees incurred by their detention. The act of 1835 is more elaborate but is substantially the same with the exception that a bond of $1,000 is required of the captain of a vessel having free negroes in its crew to guarantee their due removal, and in case the captain refuses to enter into such bond he must remove his vessel out one hundred and fifty yards from the wharf and leave port within twenty-four hours.

It was inevitable that these laws, now known as the seamen acts, would sooner or later bring the state into conflict either with other states of the union, when the control of interstate traffic by the federal government was not so common or well understood as it is today; or it would bring the state, or rather the federal government, into international difficulties with foreign governments. The state had a clear and from its point of view not unintelligent policy of police precaution. But it was not reasonable to expect other nations or even other sections of the union to see it in that light. For them to see or hear of a member of their crew, probably a citizen or subject, led off to jail with not even the semblance of a charge against him—the only answer apparently being "he is black"—was bound to call forth protest. To South Carolina it meant a police regulation; to the outside trader it meant unwarranted restriction of trade privileges.

Apparently the first month of the new year, 1823, saw wholesale arrests of such seamen at the ports, in one case not a single person was left to guard the vessel in the absence of the captain. Among the number was a colored seaman, Peter Petrie, one of the crew of the British liner, Marmion. Petrie was a subject of His Majesty the King of England. The British consul at Charleston made formal protest and reported the facts to his home government, which in turn made complaint to the government at Washington. President Monroe referred the matter to Attorney General Wirt for an opinion. This opinion, rendered May 8, 1824, took the ground that South Carolina had no such power to regulate and interfere with foreign and interstate commerce, this power resting solely with the federal government; in addition to this the United States had a trade agreement with Great Britain which did not stipulate that any such restrictions should be placed. This opinion, together with all the papers, was transmitted to Governor Wilson of South Carolina. The latter submitted them in the fall to the legislature with a message upholding the rights of the state to pass such regulations for its protection from a class of persons whose condition is dangerous to its well-being, as it would have to protect itself against infectious disease. The state senate and house of representatives each passed a different set of resolutions, the house having laid the senate resolutions on the table, upholding the state's policy, while those of the latter pointed out that the law is in no sense a commercial regulation but a police measure and could not be repealed. In the words of a newspaper correspondent, "the whole matter rests precisely in the state where it was before it had been brought to the view of the legislature."

Apparently at about the same time another line of action was taken up by the British government, namely to go into the federal courts to test the validity of the South Carolina laws on the subject. At first Judge Johnson requested that the case be taken to the state courts believing that they would correct the evil complained of. Whether or not this was done, it was later entered in the Federal District Court as "Ex parte Henry Elkison, a subject of His Brittanic Majesty, vs. Francis Delisieseline, sheriff of Charleston District," and a decision was rendered in August 7, 1823. Judge Johnson, a native of Charleston, says of the law in his decision:

"Upon the whole I am decidedly of opinion that the 3rd section of the State Act now under consideration is unconstitutional and void and that every arrest made under it subjects the parties making it to an action of trespass." His opinion, however, was that habeas corpus rested with the state to be granted and that in the absence of positive congressional enactment he as federal judge was powerless to render relief.

Again, in 1830, Daniel Fraser, a colored subject of the King of England was arrested by the sheriff of Charleston under the provisions of this act. The British consul wrote a note to the sheriff couched in considerate language, stating that he appreciated the difficulties under which the people of the state labored, but added that it had happened heretofore that British subjects had been released on the representations of the home government. It is probable that the law was not strictly enforced against seamen on foreign vessels. The sheriff referred the letter to the attorney-general of the state, who replied that as much as he regretted such a state of affairs he was aware that not only was it the law but that it was the settled policy of the state that the law should be enforced, stating his reasons as follows:

"But as a member of the Legislature, I know that several efforts have been made within a few years past to relax the policy of these laws and that they all have decidedly failed. It is not more than a fortnight since I had myself the honor of reporting a bill from the Charleston delegation to relieve the commerce of Charleston of some of the embarrassments caused by these acts; but this bill too, it seems, has failed even in the House of Representatives—that branch of the Legislature hitherto most favorable to the amendments proposed." Fraser was soon afterwards released on condition that his vessel should move out from all communication with the land.

Another case occurred in 1843. A British free negro, Jim Jones, was arrested and imprisoned by the Charleston sheriff. Because he was ordered to sweep the lower floor of the jail he cursed the jailer villainously in the presence of the other colored prisoners. Governor Hammond, in his message No. 3, calls attention to the undesirability of confining negro seamen with other prisoners and recommended that the former be prohibited by law from entering the city beyond limits to be fixed by the municipal authorities. This he pointed out would obviate the objection of foreign powers to the imprisonment of parts of the crews of their vessels and still carry into effect the purpose of the former police regulations. A bill embodying the governor's recommendation passed the house of representatives by a vote of 68 to 32,—the vote of the Charleston delegation being divided 8 for and 7 against any change. It was lost in the senate by a vote of 27 to 14.

It appears that the British consul had in 1850 made formal protest to the legislature against the vigorous enforcement of the act discriminating against subjects of color of the English king and that a joint committee of both houses to whom the matter was referred recommended that no change be made.

Two more cases for British complaint arose in 1852. Manuel Pereira, a negro, was taken from a British vessel that had been driven into port by storm on March 24; again, on June 9, Reuben Roberts, a negro, in the crew of a Clyde liner, was arrested. The British government brought on legal action praying the right of habeas corpus for Pereira in the state court, but the writ was refused by Judge Withers. In behalf of Roberts a suit for damages in the amount of $4,000 against the sheriff was brought in the federal court alleging "assault and false imprisonment." These suits seem to have been friendly and were brought by the consul at the direction of his home government. The plaintiff relied upon treaties with the United States to support his complaint. The judge of the Federal District Court directed a verdict to be entered in favor of the sheriff. An appeal was taken to the Supreme

Court of the United States, but was afterwards abandoned by the British government, the costs being assumed by the plaintiff.

The other source of protest against these laws was Massachusetts. Among those who had fallen under their enforcement were free colored persons recognized as citizens of that state. In 1842 one hundred and fifty-five merchants interested in Southern trade sent a petition to congress praying for some relief from the hampering of their business by these laws. The memorial was referred to the Committee on Commerce in the House of Representatives. This committee, on January 20, 1843, brought in a majority and minority report accompanied by all the papers accumulated in the Department of State relative to the international notes passed between the United States government and the English government already referred to. The majority report, following the lines of Attorney-General Wirt's reasoning in 1823, expressed the belief that the action of South Carolina in enacting and enforcing such a law was not lawful, but declared its belief that Congress had no preventive power in the case, adding that the federal courts probably do have such power.

A minority report was made in which it was recited that the cause of such an act in South Carolina was the Vesey plot and that in other states similar danger and the incendiary activity of the abolitionists at the North had caused the enactment of similar laws ; it is denied that citizenship in Massachusetts confers citizenship in any and every other state. If the status of the person is determined by his domicile why, it is asked, does Massachusetts refuse to recognize a negro from South Carolina as a slave since that is his status there. The right of police laws to be enacted by each state to suit its own needs was inalienable— quarantine laws being used as an illustration. The minority report was accompanied by an opinion of Attorney General Berrien rendered in 1831 on the subject. The grounds of this opinion was substantially the basis of the minority report, the illustration of that of domicile was that of England instead of Massachusetts; the quarantine laws are also used as an illustration.

Massachusetts apparently was not satisfied with letting matters rest with this, and in 1843 the legislature of that state authorized the governor to appoint a representative of the state at Charleston to secure names and information concerning such negroes of that state as had been imprisoned but not charged with crime, and to bring one or more suits to test the validity of these laws. Some difficulty was encountered in securing any person either a resident of Charleston or one at home to undertake the mission. Finally the venerable Samuel Hoar, of more than three score, ventured upon the delicate task. He arrived in Charleston on November 28, 1844, while the South Carolina legislature was in session. He respectfully wrote Governor Hammond apprising him of the purpose of his mission. The latter referred the communication to the Carolina law-making body then in session with an explanation in a special message. On December 5, the House Committee on Foreign Affairs, to whom the message and letter had been referred, made its report declaring this action to be with the avowed purpose of interfering with the institutions of the state and disturbing her peace. It directed the governor to use what means were necessary for the immediate removal of Agent Hoar from the state and that these resolutions—passed with only one dissenting vote—be laid before the governor of Massachusetts. But this official action was unnecessary, for Charleston was already dealing with the situation in its own summary way. Excitement in the city was high. The sheriff, those interested in the peace of the city and friends of Mr. Hoar, called upon him urging him to withdraw, representing to him the personal danger he incurred by delay. He was loath to leave without in some measure attempting to fulfill his mission. The apparent risk grew more visible until fairly by pressure he was shown to a waiting carriage and was soon aboard a boat leaving the harbor. Thus the unpleasant incident was closed.

"Stand-pat" is a phrase that can aptly be applied to South Carolina slave legislation. The natural conservatism of the people and the sensitiveness of the slaveholding aristocracy to any attack on the institution of slavery, together with a general hesitancy of everybody to fly to dangers they might not know of, kept these laws on the statute books until 1865. In 1855 Governor Adams, in his message to the legislature, earnestly recommended the abolition of these laws, adding that the conditions under which they had been enacted had materially changed and the supremacy of the state in its police control had been fully vindicated. The only possible service they could render at this time was to call down upon the state further ill will. The Charleston Mercury of November 30, 1855, in an editorial, agreed heartily with the governor. On the other hand "A Carolina Planter" takes issue with this view in the Charleston Courier of December 8, 1855.

The Mercury within a few days comes back with this retort:

"We presume that if a count were made it would be found that every opponent of the change is a country planter or a country resident. The city does not fear the consequences of a change. It is our country friends that take the trouble to be frightened for our sake."

It is not probable, however, that the above deliverance as to the supporters of the law could have been made in the early years of its enforcement. Robert Y. Hayne, in a letter to a friend in 1824, has this to say of the seamen acts which it will be interesting to quote:

"The proceedings of our Legislature on the free negro question are certainly not very acceptable here and I think it is very much to be regretted that a tone of at least more moderation has not accompanied whatever measures were deemed necessary on the present occasion. South Carolina, I assure you, has a character to sustain and her own dignity requires that no intemperate expression, no threats of forcible resistance to the national government should ever be resorted to." Indeed it is not quite clear what class it was that moved the enactment and enforcement of the law. Judge Johnson, before referred to in this connection, said in a private letter to Secretary Adamson July 3, 1824, that there existed a "South Carolina Association" that pressed for the enactment of these laws and was providing for their enforcement. In his opinion in the Elkison case he says:

"Certain, however, it is that from that time [i. e., the time of the arrests of Jan., 1823] the prosecutions under this act were discontinued until lately revived by a voluntary association of gentlemen who have organized themselves into a society to see the laws carried into effect. . . . It is due to the State officers to remark that from the time that they have understood that this law has been complained of on the ground of its unconstitutionality and injurious effects upon our commerce and foreign relations they have shown every disposition to let it sleep."

He goes on to say that in the case in hand the state's attorney-general did not appear to defend the case but it was defended by "the Solicitor of the Association."

CHAPTER XIV. Negro Gatherings for Religious and Social Purposes

One of the things for which the ante-bellum South has been criticised in the management of her colored population was the restrictions on their religious instruction. Probably this criticism would have been made with less vigor had it been generally known that the laws which in the letter were rigid were almost entirely ignored as regards meetings for strictly religious purposes when no apprehension of insurrectionary activity was aroused. But the reason for not giving free rein even for religious meetings lay in the ever-present fear of servile insurrection. The patrol act of 1837 made it the duty of every officer of the militia to break up any meeting or cabal of negroes which might come to his notice, summoning for the purpose a necessary number of the men under his command. Similarly the law of 1740 provided that any justice of the peace on information of any meeting of negroes should order the same to disperse, summoning such aid as would be necessary. Section 43 of that act made it lawful for any white persons to arrest and punish with not more than twenty lashes each of any number of male slaves exceeding seven found travelling in the road together without a white person in their company. It is safe to conjecture in this last instance that few people in later years knew there was such a law on the statute books and would not have undertaken to enforce it if they had been aware of it unless they believed the negroes on mischief bent; and in that case a less number than seven would not have saved the group from castigation for which some legal excuse could have been found. These enactments and their abeyance illustrate the futility of trying to maintain a strict police system by law. The dominant race in the South depended more upon expediency than upon fine-spun legal enactments in their dealings with the inferior.

No one act dealt particularly with the matter of slave meetings until 1800 when a law was passed which made unlawful all assemblages of slaves and free negroes for mental instruction, even with whites present, "in a confined or secret place of meeting," behind "barred, bolted or locked doors" so as to prevent free ingress or egress from the same. All civil or military officers of the law were authorized to disperse such meetings and "if they deem it necessary" inflict twenty lashes on all free persons of color or turn them over to the constable, who, if the magistrate should so decide, might inflict like punishment. The act further prohibited all meetings of negroes for religious or mental instruction between sunset and sunrise. This latter provision interfered very seriously with the religious meetings held by the Methodist churches for the benefit of the negroes, because it often happened that, owing probably to lack of a full supply of ministers, it was convenient to hold these meetings at night. It was also a custom of this denomination to hold "class meetings," and the doors were locked to prevent needless interruption to the services of testimony. Similar meetings were held by the "class leaders" for the negroes. These would be violations of the law as it then stood. Accordingly the Methodist societies petitioned the legislature for a modification of the law of 1800. Hence as a result this act was modified in 1803 by making it unlawful for any person to break into any such meeting before 9 p. m., provided a majority of those present were white, without a warrant from a justice of the peace, unless no justice lived within three miles.

An opportunity for an interpretation of this law came in 1818 in the case of Bell vs. Graham, which arose as follows: At Shady Grove Methodist church in Fairfield district regular meetings composed of whites and blacks for religious purpose were held in daytime with open doors. The meetings were so often disturbed by the patrol that ministers refused to preach there. But a sturdy "class leader" attempted to keep up the meetings. On one occasion the patrol came and, apparently without examining the negroes to see if they held written passes, dispersed the meeting, severely whipping one negro and threatening the others. It was impossible later for either side to show whether or not a majority of those present were white. The class leader was prevailed upon to prosecute the beat captain for unwarranted disturbance of religious worship, but the grand jury refused to return a true bill against the patrol. The captain of the patrol then brought suit to recover damages for false imprisonment. In spite of the judge's direction to the contrary, the jury assessed damages to the amount of

$56.25 against the class leader, who promptly appealed to the higher court. The action of the two juries—the first in dismissing the case against the patrol, and the latter in finding a bill of damages against the class leader—is a clear indication, after allowance for possible local prejudices have been made, that the attitude of the authorities was always to give large discretion to the patrol in the administration of its duties. If, as is possible, local prejudice was partly responsible for the interruption of religious meetings, it emphasizes the careful distinctions the court would make. The points considered by the court may be summarized as follows: The right of undisturbed worship is inalienable; is the captain in this case protected by the patrol laws? Does the act of 1800 justify the patrol in disturbing the meeting? The whipping of the negro was unlawful since he was in the company of white persons. The plaintiff failed to show that there was not a majority of white persons present; the doors were not barred nor was the meeting in a "confined and secret place," nor was it after nine o'clock in the evening. Even were a majority of those present negroes the law would not apply here for the act of 1803 was passed with the purpose of lessening the severity of the law of 1800 and to legalize just such a meeting as this was:

"It would indeed, be a strange anomaly in legislation to legalize an evil, which it was their avowed intention to prevent; the act itself warrants no such construction."

The verdict of $56.25 against the class leader was set aside. It will be observed that the patrol captain, in so far as this action was concerned, went free as an officer of the law. It merely relieved the person who undertook to call the action of the patrol in question of any financial embarrassment consequent upon his prosecution of the patrol. This case had a pronounced effect upon the method and manner of the enforcement of the patrol law, and diminished the severity of its application against negro meetings. Judge O'Neall said later that the provisions of these laws prohibiting negro meetings were dead letters in so far as their enforcement was concerned. Any effort definitely by enactment to liberalize these laws or their principles met with disfavor. Several petitions with this in view were sent to the legislature. One from Sumter with particularly strong endorsement was presented in 1842 and apparently caused some discussion, but it was referred to the judiciary committee which reported unfavorably. No trace of its ever having come to a vote in any way is revealed by the Journal.

Survivors of the ante-bellum period say that the custom in the rural districts was for assemblages of negroes to meet occasionally on Sunday afternoons for religious worship and instruction and if one white person was present who was responsible for the conduct of the negroes that were present with their written passes, even if the negroes conducted the services, all the requirements of the sentiments of the community were considered satisfied. Where the slaves did not greatly outnumber the whites, as was the case on the up-country farms, a gallery or the rear of the church was set apart for the exclusive use of such of the slaves as cared to attend the services held for the whites. Sometimes there were meetings held for the negroes just after the service for the whites, when no white persons other than the minister were present. There appears to have been no objection on the part of masters to any preaching to their slaves unless there was reason to believe that the person exercising this privilege was hostile to the institution of slavery or would inculcate in the minds of the slaves disturbing ideas that would tend to render them discontented with their condition. Harrison, in his "Gospel Among the Slaves," indicates that the slave owners were glad to have preaching for their slaves since it increased the ease of control.

On the other hand the Southern whites were ever alert to prevent incendiary preaching to their slaves, as is shown in the following quotation from a pamphlet by "A Carolinian" published in 1823 while the attempted Charleston insurrection was fresh in people's minds :

"Our planters have just cause of complaint on this subject [i. e., of negro meetings]. It is known to many that field negroes have been collected and addressed without the knowledge and consent of their masters. The planters, however, are now alive to their duty, and their interests, and it is not probable that such highly censurable conduct will ever be repeated."

The Society for the Propagation of the Gospel in Foreign Parts was chartered by William III in 1701. Within about a half a century of this time it had established a school for negroes in Charleston. This effort, under the auspices of the Episcopal Church, was perhaps the earliest and until the close of the Revolutionary War, the most effective effort to reach the colored population. There are contained in the instructions to the missionaries specific directions as to dealing with the negroes.

Some efforts had been made by others soon afterwards, if not contemporaneously. The Methodists reported 890 colored members in 1796 and by 1821 they numbered 42,059. The Baptists in 1806 reported 3,500. In 1819 it is estimated that one-fourth of the communicants of the Presbyterian churches of Charleston were colored.

It was about this time, 1828, that C. C. Pinckney went to the Rev. Mr. William Capers (afterwards bishop) and asked if he could secure for him a Methodist exhorter as an overseer, he having heard that one such had been a decided success on a friend's plantation owing to the fact that the overseer had relied more upon the religious motive than the lash as an incentive to good behavior. Capers was not slow to see the opportunity and while he was not in a position to supply him with such an overseer, he offered to send a "missionary" to preach to the slaves on his plantation, to which Pinckney readily assented. Such is the well authenticated story connected with the founding of the Methodist missions to the slaves in South Carolina in 1828, of which Capers became the first superintendent.

We shall have to drop the incidents of the work begun and carried forward by the denominations, though interesting, to study the complications to which it in part gave rise.

Soon after this promising beginning in efforts to improve the colored race began the publication of abolitionist literature in the North and the terrible Nat Turner insurrection in Virginia. This halted all benevolent movements for the betterment of the negroes' status. It is clearly put by Rev. C. C. Jones, a Presbyterian minister, who had devoted his life to work for the negro in Georgia:

"The very foundations of society were assailed and men went forth to the defense. A tenderness was begotten in the public mind on the whole subject, and every movement touching the improvement of the negroes was watched with jealousy.

"It was considered best to disband schools and discontinue meetings at least for a season; the formation of societies and the action of ecclesiastical bodies in some degree ceased.

"The feelings of men being excited, those who had undertaken the religious instruction of the negroes were looked upon with suspicion and some of them were obliged to quit the field. It was not considered that a separation could be made between the religious and civil condition of the people; and that a minister could confine himself to the one without interfering at all with the other."

But not all hope was given up by benevolently disposed whites after the excitement had quieted down. There is in the Charleston Library a pamphlet publishing the proceedings in part of a meeting called to assemble in Charleston May 13-15, 1845, to discuss and plan for a more intelligent and systematic religious instruction of the slave population. It was promoted apparently by the Episcopalian churches, chiefly those of Charleston, while the other denominations contributed their part to the movement. A series of letters had been sent out to a number of ministers and planters in all parts of the state making inquiry as to the present status of the religious instruction of the negroes, as to how often meetings were held for them, and if these were conducted by negroes solely. Other questions were asked, but these indicate the phase of the subject in which we are interested. The replies form the more interesting part of the pamphlet, showing religious conditions and the customs among the negroes to be very much as they have been described above. It seems that the difficulties that would attend any modification of the law so as to allow more liberty for religious meetings of the negroes remained unsolved and the meeting adjourned without being able to arrive at any satisfactory conclusion along this line.

One point brought out clearly in the replies is that the services of the negro preachers to their own race were considered inexpedient. In some instances the colored preachers were commended but in most they were condemned as being ignorant and incapable of giving intelligent instruction even if they did not teach ideas subversive of the established order of things. Russell, in his Diary, quotes a white man in Georgetown as saying that these negro preachers "do the niggers no good—they talk about things going on elsewhere and get their minds unsettled and so on." The report of a committee appointed by the South Carolina Agricultural Society to investigate the religious instruction of the slave recommends against allowing negroes to preach. Some whites even objected to the negro "watchman," whose duty it was to look after the spiritual welfare of the slaves associated with him, because, they claimed, it gave them undue prominence and undue self-conceit as a result.

While the negro preacher was tolerated and probably accomplished much good in many instances, it was the possibility of the harm he might do that disturbed the whites. The religious meeting composed solely of blacks was looked upon with more decided disfavor and was probably rare. Here are some characteristic remarks about such a meeting in Charleston in 1816:

"Almost every night there is a meeting of these noisy, frantic worshippers. . . . Midnight! Is that the season for religious convocation? Even allowing that these meetings were conducted with propriety, is that the accepted time? That the meeting of numerous black people to hear the scripture expounded by an ignorant and (too frequently) vicious person of their own color can be of no benefit either to themselves or the community is certain; that it may be attended with many evils is, I presume, obvious to every reflecting mind." It had always been the separate meeting of blacks under their own management that had aroused most suspicion in the mind of the public. Jervey, in his "Life and Times of Robert Y. Hayne," mentions two such meetings. At one in 1817 four hundred and sixty-nine negroes were arrested in Charleston for holding a meeting in a house and on a lot owned by the negroes. The other is quoted from the Charleston Courier of June 9, 1818. It is important enough to be quoted in full:

"One hundred and forty free Negroes and Slaves, belonging to the African church, were taken up on Sunday afternoon by the City Guard and lodged in the guard-house. The city council yesterday morning sentenced five of them, consisting of a Bishop and four ministers, to one month's imprisonment, or to give security to leave the state. Bright other ministers were also sentenced separately to receive ten lashes or pay a fine each of ten dollars." On the other hand it will be interesting to note that it was the official policy of at least a part of the Presbyterian Church to have their ministers hold separate meetings for the negroes, but this was different from the negroes conducting their own meeting. James L. Pettigru is quoted as saying in a speech at the meeting on the Religious Instruction of the Negroes that the sentiment for separate meetings for the negroes was growing.

Certain free negroes of Charleston petitioned the legislature in 1820 to be permitted to conduct their own worship independently at Hampstead, their church having been already erected. The matter was referred to the Charleston delegation in the general assembly, who recommended unfavorable action upon the petition.

It was brought out at the Vesey trial that it was at an "African congregation [which] was not only composed of colored persons but their minister was also colored" that the details of the plot were worked out.

Sometime prior to 1850 there was a church in Charleston for negro worship called Calvary, founded under the direction and authority of the Protestant Episcopal Church of South Carolina, probably because there was no adequate accommodation for them in the churches for white people. This colored congregation seems to have aroused some question in the people's minds as to the expediency and lawfulness of such a venture. Such was the feeling that a public meeting was held, over which the mayor presided, to inquire into the matter. Committees were appointed to investigate: (1) What measures for the religious instruction of negroes were used in Charleston and with what results, good or bad—if bad, how could they be remedied ; (2) All the material facts bearing on the particular case of Calvary church; (3) What the laws governing such a case are, and is the enactment of other laws desirable? The important points brought out by the inquiry were that the church was organized by the Episcopal Church, for there was not sufficient accommodation for the people of color as was the case in many other places. The church had been placed under a regularly authorized minister of that denomination; the teaching was oral. There was a place set apart for whites who might care to attend either for precaution as to the movements of the negroes or for any other reason. There were found to exist "bands" among the negroes the purpose of which was to relieve the sick and assist in the expenses incurred in the burial of their dead. The burial society was a sort of fraternal necessity for free negroes and slaves in the towns who were allowed to hire their time and act in a large measure as free. But the very name and the possibilities suggested by its nature would arouse suspicion. The Reverend Whiteford Smith, of the Methodist Church, who participated in the meeting, came to the defense of the "bands," attesting their benevolent character. No further definite action as to the Calvary church appears to have been taken.

Negro funerals were almost always held at night, in order probably to accommodate slaves who could at this time only have opportunity to attend them. An ordinance of the city of Charleston in 1789 prohibiting the meeting at a free negro's house of more than seven slaves made an exception in the case of funerals, with a view apparently of encouraging the custom. A rather weird sight must have been this racially superstitious people carrying torches with the corpse, and the laying to rest one of their number often with more or less curious ceremonies. Probably the whites, trusting to the semi-barbarous superstition of the negroes being awed by the presence of death, allowed these funerals, thinking of no possible harm to come from them. But if we are to believe the account of a "Taxable Citizen of Ward Four," who writes to the Southern Patriot of September 19, 1835, even these funerals are fraught with danger and are something more than solemn:

"There are sometimes every evening in the week funerals of negroes accompanied by three or four hundred negroes and a tumultuous crowd of other slaves who disturb all the other inhabitants in the neighborhood of burying grounds in Pitt street near Boundary street. It appears to be a jubilee for every slave in the city. They are seen eagerly pressing to the place from all quarters, and such is frequently the crowd and noise made by them that carriages cannot safely be driven that way. . . . Let it be remembered too that the officiating priests are black men." The article recommends that attendance at negro funerals be limited by ordinance to fifteen or twenty composed only of relatives of the deceased and that the guard be instructed to take up all hangers-on.

It appears that at times, after proper precautions had been taken, some social privileges were allowed the slaves by their masters. The celebrations of weddings were not unusual things. Even dances were doubtless permitted. But the more common form of social privilege allowed was in the nature of bringing the slaves together and under the glow of the hilarity that comes of social contact they were set to light tasks. Log rolling, when a neighbor invites the slaves of other owners in the community to assemble at a not very busy season to assist in getting off the newly cleared land the timber and debris, was one of these occasions. Feats and contests of strength afforded merriment. A dinner, plentiful if not elaborate, crowned the event. "Corn shuckings" to which all the slaves in the community were invited were common, even weekly occurrences in the harvesting time. After the corn was all husked supper would be served; sometimes whiskey too, in the yard by the light of the moon, and various matches as wrestling were engaged in, and the negro melodies resounded, after which the crowd broke up and went home, refreshed by the outlet afforded their spirits. The slaveowners and whites generally did not object to the slave attending religious services or having the privilege of some social enjoyment. It was the constant danger they felt, perhaps often exaggerated, of the meetings being made the occasion of insurrectionary activity. This is the reason for the acts of 1800 and 1839 expressly prohibiting such meetings, which if they had been rigidly observed and enforced would well-nigh have cut off all opportunity of the negroes to meet together for any purpose. Booker Washington thinks that the restrictions obtained were sufficient to prevent the financial progress of the free negroes in the state, and had there not been such restrictions on their co-operation facilitated by meetings held by them in their interest they would have been further advanced in 1861 than they were. The patrol was given the authority to interfere in these meetings. And, notwithstanding the tendency which existed, of giving the patrol large discretionary powers, we see how that in 1818 the patrol was rebuked by the highest court for interference in a religious meeting.

Another case, the State vs. Boozer et al., from Newberry district, came up to the Court of Appeals from the lower court in 1850. This decision puts a liberal interpretation on the law regarding innocent meetings of negroes for other than religious edification. The main facts are, that not far from what is now Prosperity a slave woman secured the consent of her master to hold a "quilting," to invite other slaves and to use the master's kitchen for the purpose. Less than a dozen slaves, a majority being women, were present with written passes from their masters. Everything was orderly and went well until after the master, in whose kitchen the meeting took place, had retired. About eleven o'clock he was aroused by a disturbance, caused by the presence of the patrol. The captain of the patrol was remonstrated with by the master all to no purpose. The master was ordered to summon all his slaves from the kitchen while the others were whipped by the patrol although they produced their passes. The owners of some of the visiting slaves decided to test the matter in the courts. The patrol was prosecuted and fined $25 in the sessions court for "unlawfully whipping slaves." The patrol appealed on the ground that it was a meeting of negroes after 9 p. m. and that there were no whites present except the resident master and his family who were asleep in the dwelling house some distance away. It was clear that the patrol had from the letter of the law a good defense. But the court took the opposite view and confirmed the lower court in the conviction of the patrol. Justice Withers, in giving the opinion of the court, has but little to say of the law in the case and bases his decision more on expediency and the general principles of a generous humanity and the implied purpose of the slave code. Indeed the way in which the letter of the law is evaded is rather remarkable, but it was not unusual in this highest tribunal to take such liberal views on the interpretation of the slave law even to such an extent that the judges were criticised for it. The court was careful to say that had there been reasonable suspicion that the meeting was of a disturbing or disorderly kind the patrol would have been upheld completely. But the presumption was all the other way. The court says in part:

"The slaves who were whipped were on the premises of a citizen, himself a slaveowner, by his consent, and with tickets from their masters. The occasion was a perfectly innocent one, even meritorious; for Hunter's negro women had obtained his permission to call in the assistance toward the construction of a quilt for her bed, or some bed; and it is to be hoped that no master in the state would have denied such an indulgence, when he had no motive to suspect that it was contrived to cover up some evil design. How many of us have permitted to our slaves the enjoyment of a wedding party and ceremony in imitation of the higher classes, and even contributed to the good cheer of the occasion? It is surely no novelty among slaveowners, that by consent of all parties, one slave should obtain the assistance of his neighbors to gather his little crop, even though it be on Saturday night, or to erect or improve his cabin. It would be painful to find that the law forbids masters to permit or encourage the slave in honoring the humble virtues that may be consistent with his condition, whether the same take the direction of social relations and intercourse among themselves, or the advancement of household comforts. The true spirit of our law does not aim at such an end, where the mode of attaining it presents no conflict with the interests, peace and security of the public. These must undoubtedly be regarded at all hazards; and no police regulations subserving that high policy can be justly branded as cruel or tyrannical.

"It would seem simply ridiculous to suppose that the safety of the State or any of its inhabitants, was implicated in such an assemblage as this at Hunter's, composed of a few males, more females; with tickets from their owners; in the kitchen of a citizen by his consent; not impudent or disorderly by the admission of the defendants, assembled at a quilting and no evidence of a carousal by eating or drinking. "Let them [i. e., the patrol] exercise with judicious freedom the power to disperse unlawful assemblies as they are expressly empowered by . . . the patrol law to do, in relation to slaves, free negroes and mustizoes; such for example as are found in disorderly houses . . . but a judicious freedom in the administration of our police laws for the lower order must always have respect to the confidence which the law reposes in the discretion of the master, the presence of the proprietor, his loyalty to the sympathies and the policy, involves our common interests, peace and safety."

CHAPTER XV. Slave Insurrections

The following paragraph will narrate some instances of well-known insurrectionary attempts that may be found treated in other accounts of slavery. However, their mention here will not only serve to complete the description of the police control of the slaves, but will at the same time show what basis there was for the great fear which the whites continually felt in varying degrees of intensity. It is the explanation of the stringency of some slave laws, particularly those just discussed prohibiting meetings of negroes, sometimes to the extent of interfering with religious instruction.

The danger from insurrection seems to have been imminent from early times since almost the first act on slavery, that of 1690, provided the death penalty for an attempt to instigate an uprising. As a precaution the act of 1722 made it the duty of justice of the peace to seize any horses kept solely by slaves since they afforded additional opportunity for the carrying on of insurrectionary plots.

The first plot of much importance was the Stono uprising of September 9, 1739. The Spanish colony at St. Augustine, always hostile to the South Carolina settlement, seems to have encouraged in every way the incendiary propensities of the South Carolina slaves. McCrady, whose account is for the most part followed here, says that the slaves were encouraged by emissaries of the Spanish to leave their masters and on reaching the Spanish fort were protected and even organized into militia companies; and these facts were communicated to other slaves in Carolina to encourage them also to leave. A number of negroes finally assembled at Stono, broke open a warehouse, killed the two guards, stole the arms and ammunition, and proceeding further, killed a Mr. Godfrey and family and fired his house. For fifteen miles they proceeded burning, plundering and murdering, compelling all negroes they met to follow. Twenty-one white persons fell victims to their barbarism. Finding rum in some of the houses, they imbibed freely with the result that they began to celebrate with an orgy of dance and song.

Governor Bull met them on his return from a visit to the outside. A Mr. Golightly had also observed them from a safe distance. These two spread the alarm, the latter pressing immediately after them on securing the assistance of the white men who were attending worship at a Presbyterian church, and who in obedience to law had gone to church armed. The militia surrounded the rebellious negroes and captured nearly all of them. Those who apparently had followed because of pressure were pardoned. Those losing their lives in the attack and those of the negroes executed amounted to forty-four.

The outbreak brought consternation to the peaceful inhabitants of the colony. The militia patrol to the southward was strengthened. In 1740 the great slave act was passed, which remained the basic negro law for the next century and a quarter. It would not be surprising then if on investigation this code should be found to be severe. Such is not the case, however. McCrady states that in some respects the condition of the slaves was ameliorated. The precautions against insurrection, however, were rigid, one section prohibiting beating drums, blowing horns or the like which might on occasion be used to arouse slaves to insurrectionary activity. A special act of the same year was passed quieting any claim against the state by any owner for a slave who had been put to death by execution for being concerned in the insurrection.

The City Gazette and Daily Advertiser (Charleston) of November 22, 1797, tells of four negroes being tried on the charge of conspiracy to fire the city of Charleston. One turned state's evidence against the others. This one with one of the others was sentenced to be transported, while the other two went to the scaffold. Five days later another was implicated and hanged. It was perhaps merely an isolated case of a purpose or possibly a threat of incendiarism and may not have been serious in its extent and aim. But it illustrates the possibilities involved.

Some fear apparently had come to be had of unprincipled and irresponsible whites who for any reason might aid in insurrectionary movements. The act of 1805 made it treason punishable with death for "any person" in any way to aid in an insurrection. Confession or the testimony of two witnesses was sufficient to convict. Good reason for believing that this was intended to reach whites is that no such limitations as to evidence would be probable in the case of a negro.

The Camden attempt at insurrection occurred in 1816. The betrayal of the plot led the whites to believe that it had been in contemplation for a long time. The plan was to fire the "powder magazine," an old arsenal, thus attracting the attention of the white people to that part of the town while the negroes should assemble in another quarter, massacre the whites and burn the rest of the town. They had apparently, as was usually the case except in the Vesey instance, nothing further definitely in view. The date for the attempt was significantly set for July 4. A faithful slave revealed the plot to his master who communicated with the governor. An officer of the militia was detailed to secure evidence of the plot, without if possible revealing the identity of the informing slave. By a shrewd move Col. Chestnut carried on a counter plot and in this way secured the details of the original plot. Seventeen were arrested, seven of whom were convicted after a trial before a court consisting of two magistrates and five freeholders. Five were executed; one was pardoned after all the plans for his execution had been completed; one was sentenced to one year's imprisonment or to be deported from the United States. The informing slave was purchased by an act of the legislature appropriating $1,100 for the purpose and giving to the slave $50 per annum during his lifetime. This insurrectionary effort seems to have put Camden and the up-country on their guard, for the act of 1818 on the Camden patrol shows an increased interest and vigilance.

But the attempt at insurrection which is the best known as one of the more important plots in the United States, and which showed more intelligence in its conception and plan, was the Vesey plot of 1822 in Charleston. Denmark Vesey, a free negro, planned it in conjunction with certain slaves, the more important of whom were Gullah Jack, Monday Gell and Peter Poyas. The plan was for those in the plot to rise suddenly about the first of July, seize the shipping, burn the town, and then sail away to the West Indies. The slaves invited to join were told that the whites were contemplating a gigantic slaughter of the negroes because they had become too numerous. Everything was apparently in readiness for some time. On May 30, Peter, a faithful slave who had been asked to join the plot, communicated what he knew to his master. The city authorities were apprised, a court summoned, and information sought. Arrests were made, and, to show the persistence of the leaders, even after some of those involved had been arrested, they either in desperation or without fully calculating the determination of the whites made efforts to bring the plot into execution. But the greater part of them were intimidated. The special negro court of magistrates and freeholders sat almost continuously for nearly a month. Those first arrested were placed in solitary confinement, and as the trial proceeded confessions came out, some after the prisoners had been sentenced to be hanged. The number arrested was 131, 67 of whom were convicted; the number executed was 35, all slaves except Vesey; the number deported, 32. In the appendix to Kennedy & Parker's Negro Plot, p. 189, is related the trial and conviction of four white men in the session court for complicity in the plot. Their sentences ranged from three to twelve months' imprisonment and upon release they were to be required to give security for good behavior for five years in sums ranging from $100 to $1,000.

The Nat Turner insurrection in Virginia in 1831 aroused the whole South. Every community in near proximity beat the bushes, as a local phrase puts it, to see if there were any additional plots subsidiary to the greater one in Virginia. There is little or nothing to indicate that the South Carolina slaves were in any way concerned. However, in Laurens district two slaves were tried and convicted of being in an agreement to meet others and to join in such an undertaking if the opportunity should arise. The Nashville Republican and State Gazette of October 22, 1831, copies a letter from the Baltimore Chronicle to the effect that it was believed that the Turner plot was widespread and that an attack on Cheraw had been planned. Chapman relates a reminiscence that at one time there was great excitement at the town of Newberry aroused by a rumor that a number of negroes had made an outbreak near Jalapa, seven miles distant, but it turned out to be a mere hoax. These are sufficient to show in how dangerous a situation the people of the South believed themselves to be. Probably, it is not, therefore, too much to say that their fears were exaggerated.

The Vesey plot put everybody to thinking. The fancied security of the whites, if it existed, had a rude awakening. Everybody was anxious that some remedy should be applied, but were perhaps doubtful of what it should be. Citizens of Charleston presented a memorial to the legislature praying the expulsion of free negroes from the state. Indeed, because Vesey was free and because he was not a native of the state great distrust of the free negroes arose, and particularly did the people appear to think that every precaution should be taken to keep any of this class from coming into the state. Since several strengthenings of the slave law had already been accomplished in the three years just preceding—as a new patrol law and one prohibiting further manumission—the only direction in which further improvements could be effected was in a stricter enforcement of the laws, and passing of the seamen acts. But the extreme precaution taken against immigrant free persons of color in the seamen act threatened to cause international complications. As Professor Phillips suggests, the Vesey plot checked any tendency toward liberalism which may have been prevalent at this time and made the arguments of the abolitionists which began to be disseminated within the next decade, the less acceptable to the South.

138

CHAPTER XVI. Abolition and Incendiary Literature

It will now be easier to see why the South looked with hostility upon abolition and abolition propagandists as enemies of the established order of things. They regarded the slave stealer as a sort of anarchist, but understood his motives. But to the South the abolitionist appeared as a red-handed murderer and worse. Perhaps there was some reason for it, indeed from their way of looking at it very good reason. Slavery was not only an economic and industrial system, and as such felt to be a burden by the non-slaveholder; but more than that, it was a gigantic police system, which the poor man in the up-country as well as the wealthy planter in the lowlands did not know how to replace. To put the negro on an equality with the white man politically, if considered at all, was regarded as madness. Now the abolitionist program was for the most part negative—away with the institution of slavery! To the mind of Southerners abolitionist literature and teaching would excite undue hopes in the minds of the slaves. Naturally they would turn to assist the propaganda with the torch and crude implements of murder and torture. It rendered unsafe the homes and farms scattered over the state. The natural instincts of social self-preservation revolted at any faith, belief or movement that had as its filial principle the sudden overturning of the established order of society. The editor of the Camden Journal on November 23, 1833, replied in an editorial to the request of Dennison for an exchange of his paper for the Emancipator by asking "if he would exchange courtesies with a ruthless incendiary who should enter his dwelling at midnight with a flaming torch and fixed determination to spread ruin and desolation? Let his answer be ours." In 1820 a law was enacted making it a high misdemeanor with a maximum punishment of a fine of $1,000 and imprisonment for a year for any white person to introduce into the state any written or printed matter subversive of the established order of things with reference to slavery. Any free negro found guilty of the same was to pay the above fine; for the second offense he was to receive fifty lashes and be banished from the state. If he returned, unless by unavoidable accident, the penalty was death. An act of 1823 prohibited, under penalty of a fine of $1,000, the bringing into the state by any person as a servant any free negro who had been in the West Indies, Mexico or South America, or any of the states north of the Potomac, or in the city of Washington. The fear was that free negro servants so travelled would be dangerous if brought into contact with the slaves.

About 1831, at the time of the beginning of the abolitionist activity at the North and after a few of their papers had found their way to the South, there appeared in the Southern Times and State Gazette of October 8, 1831, published at Columbia, the following significant card:

"$1,500 REWARD

"The Vigilance Association, composed of a body of gentlemen of the first respectability, offers a reward of Fifteen Hundred Dollars for the apprehension and prosecution to conviction, of any white person who may be detected in distributing or circulating within this state, the newspaper called 'The Liberator,' printed in Boston by Garrison and Knapp—or the pamphlet called the 'Walker Pamphlet'—or any other publication of a similar and equally mischievious and seditious tendency. Signed by the authority and in behalf of the Association

"Columbia, S. C., Sept. 29, 1831."

Governor Hamilton, in message No. 2 to the legislature in 1831, in speaking of the Southampton insurrection, quoted the governor of Virginia to the effect that these abolition papers had probably been the moving cause of the uprising. He then referred to the fact that the city authorities of Savannah had written the authorities of Boston with a view to having the publication suppressed, but the latter had replied that they had no power to comply. Probably the best way to deal with the incendiary literature would have been to turn over to the federal government its control. But Southerners scouted the idea since they feared the rights of the state would be too much interfered with.

The refusal to consider any plan to put in the hands of the federal government the matter of dealing with incendiary publications made it impossible for the state to punish even indirectly those outside who sent incendiary publications into the state. Hence they undertook to deal in their own way with this literature after it was brought into the state. The Charleston Courier, on July 30, 1835, referred in a news note to the fact that a considerable quantity of abolitionist literature had been received at the Charleston post office for distribution. The postmaster promised some persons interested in peace and order not to distribute the matter until the postoffice department could be heard from. But on the following night other persons openly and forcibly entered the office and removed the objectionable literature. A citizens' meeting was called by the town council for the following Monday. This meeting seems not to have taken into consideration so much the lawless action of those entering the postoffice—probably regarding it as a consequence to be expected—as removing the occasion for such actions in the future. It appears that Robert Y. Hayne's influence prevented a vote of approval of the lawless act of the mob. By resolution a committee of twenty-one was appointed to take such action as was thought best. This committee conferred with the postmaster and obtained from him a promise that no incendiary literature thereafter received at the postoffice should be distributed until the city authorities should be notified of its presence; the committee appointed a sub-committee to accompany the next mail from the wharf to the office to prevent violence. Thus closed a disagreeable incident though the fundamental questions at stake were far from a satisfactory understanding.

As will appear from the following quotation from the Laurensville Herald of August 24, 1849, it seems that incendiary matter had been sent through the upper part of the state:

"ABOLITION DOCUMENTS

"These incendiary publications, as we learn from the Pendleton Messenger, are still sent in large quantities through Anderson and Pickens districts. They are not distributed, however, but consigned to the flames by the postmasters as soon as opened. How much longer will our people submit to be thus insulted?" Public attention was soon given to the matter at Pendleton resulting in an incident similar to that at Charleston. In 1849 a group of persons were at the postoffice receiving their mail when one present was handed a piece of unpalatable literature, and proceeded to read it for the edification of those present. Upon inquiry it was found that there were thirty-eight more such papers. The local vigilance committee already organized demanded the objectionable matter. The postmaster refused to give it to anyone except those to whom it was directed. The newspaper narrative of the incident describes it further as follows:

"The committee told him [the postmaster] they were determined to have the papers peaceably if they could, forcibly they must, that resistance would be in vain. They then entered the office, shoved the postmaster aside and took possession of them and now have them under lock and key." No further notice of the matter appears and this probably was the end of it.

Amos Kendall, postmaster-general, had taken a rather two-sided stand on slavery literature, to the effect that he had no power to prevent transmission of objectionable matter in the mails nor to protect it from violence. A series of resolutions were passed by the legislature of South Carolina in December, 1835, declaring abolition societies subversive of the union, calling upon non-slaveholding states to aid in their suppression and commending the attitude of the federal government toward the mails.

About this time began the controversial arguments over the merits and demerits of slavery, carried on through pamphlets and otherwise. They called forth the best intellectual talent of the South, but instead of bringing those in the North holding views different from those held in the South closer together it served further to separate them. But the controversial side of slavery does not come within the scope of this paper.

There were at times, particularly after 1830, and during the last decade of the slavery period, extra-legal committees and associations organized for dealing both with questions of domestic policy and with outside interference with slavery. In Sumter district, in 1850, there was organized a "Southern Rights Associations," with a "vigilance committee." This committee was to watch for any appearance of outside interference with the slaves, to report and prosecute cases of illegal trafficking or selling liquor to negroes. A similar association and committee existed in Kershaw district. These are typical.

In 1849 a white man was indicted for circulating incendiary papers in Spartanburg district and held to trial under a bond for $1,000. Counsel complained that he had won considerable unpopularity by taking the case. The papers in the case are preserved in the county clerk of court's office at Spartanburg. With them is preserved a pamphlet, "An address to South Carolinians," by "Brutus," presumably one of the objectionable publications, although it refers but little to slavery and is chiefly an appeal to the poor whites to demand a larger participation in public affairs. The Abbeville Banner of May 27, 1858, gives a news account of a meeting held at that place to order a family to leave who were suspected of inciting the negroes to unlawful acts. Within a few days the head of the family, claiming to be a map seller, left after being waited on by a committee.

But a more general and systematic effort to prevent incendiarism came after the whole South was shaken by the John Brown raid at Harper's Ferry in 1859. Perhaps the danger from incendiaries or from the outside generally was greatly exaggerated. The immediate danger was not so great possibly as the excitement caused by the raid would seem to indicate. This emphasizes the tense feeling caused by a quarter of a century of agitation. Resolutions condemnatory of Brown in particular and of the abolitionists in general and calling for a fine-tooth-comb investigation in every community for abolitionists, by enthusiastic committees, were adopted by numerous mass meetings and sometimes by legally constituted bodies. Three illustrative instances will suffice. In Sumter district resolutions were passed of which the following form a part, calling upon the town council "to institute a rigid surveillance on all such transient persons (stragglers from the North to visit and tarry in our town as agents for books, medicines, etc., whose real object may be to act as spies and abolition emissaries) and when full satisfaction is not given to notify such persons that their presence in our community is not to be tolerated." On Nov. 25, 1859, a meeting was held in Abbeville to investigate certain suspicious characters in the community. As a result six white persons were told to leave town who promised to comply but failed to do so. They were watched and being accused of holding improper language to slaves they were arrested. At a subsequent meeting it was determined to appoint a vigilance committee to "observe the conduct of suspicious persons in the community and that they endeavor to detect any illicit traffic with slaves." On December 1, 1859, the town council of Newberry passed a preamble and resolutions of which the following definite plan is a part:

"Resolved by the Town Council of Newberry that a Vigilance Committee consisting of five gentlemen be hereby appointed and constituted, whose duty it shall be to watch the movements of strangers coming within our midst, and when they think proper to demand of such persons a reasonable account of themselves, and if, upon examination of such parties, that the said Vigilance Committee be and the same are hereby empowered to take such steps in the premises, by writs or otherwise, as they may deem proper to protect the public interests." The tense excitement in the state continued through the following year. Newberry district appears to have been well organized before the close of the next year with township associations. Of these the one in Beth Eden township is typical. The purpose of the meeting was stated to be, to secure organization throughout the state for protection against incendiaries. A committee appointed to draft resolutions made its report. Among the things recommended and that those present pledged themselves to, were: to enforce strictly patrol riding; not to give "general passes"; each owner to prevent his slaves from trading; to prevent any negro from preaching, and not to allow any negro meetings for religious purposes unless twelve white men are present; to deal legally with negro traders; to call upon the guardians of certain free negroes (named) that they be removed from the community; to allow no hunting by slaves or free negroes on the plantations. Similar sub-associations are reported from other townships and they passed similar resolutions, large numbers of slaveowners signing the paper.

What was happening in Newberry was only typical of what was going on with a greater or less degree of excitement in other parts of the state. A peddler from Philadelphia was told to move on by the vigilance committee of York. A "clean shaven" transient man at Granville turned out to be an abolitionist. The Charleston Courier of Dec. 22, 1859, quotes the Marion Star for its authority that an Englishman received a coat of tar and feathers in Columbia in complement to his abolition views. Indeed, strangers were scanned with suspicion it would often seem. Northern birth or residence not infrequently placed the burden of proof of a wholesome faith in the Southern institution upon the person so unfortunate as to have had such a former habitat.

To supplement the laws against incendiaries an act of 1859 was duly passed providing for the imposition of a fine in any amount and imprisonment for a term in the discretion of the court for any person printing, writing, drawing or engraving any paper calculated to incite slaves to insurrection. On the release of such an offender the court was to have the power to require bond for his future good behavior. The same penalties were made to apply to any one attempting to circulate such literature or subscribing for such literature with a view to distributing it. One section of the act attempted to make it the duty of the postmaster to notify the magistrate of any person receiving such literature in their mail—a provision that probably was without force.

The Kingstree incident is one of the best illustrations of the distrust felt for the Northern sojourner in the South. The services of two teachers from the North had been engaged by persons in the community. One of the teachers had been a resident of the community for about two years, and the other for a shorter period of time. On November 2, 1859, a mass meeting was held in a country store in Boggy Swamp, a few miles out from Kingstree, the courthouse seat of Williamsburg district, with a view to taking Inaction with reference to the citizens from the North sojourning in their midst. Resolutions were passed that it was the sense of those present that the two young men should be asked to leave as a precaution since they might prove eventually to be abolitionists. The newspaper account of the proceedings says:

"Nothing definite is known of their abolition or insurrectionary sentiments, but being from the North and therefore necessarily imbued with doctrines hostile to our institutions, their presence in this section has been obnoxious and at any rate suspicious." From other accounts it appears that they had received printed matter through the mail on the wrapper of which were strange markings, written by someone while the mail was en route, whether by the postmaster whence it came as a warning to the local office regarding insufficient postage or as a warning to the addressee for receiving such mail, was not clear. At a second meeting one of those present referred to the conduct of certain negroes as being very suspicious. Another prominent gentleman took the ground "that there was no positive proof" against the teachers and hence they ought to go undisturbed. A committee of twelve was appointed to communicate with the teachers and order them to leave the community. More conservative men, including the employers of the teachers, deprecated summary action, and the latter even offered to defend them against any violence. Furthermore they claimed that the young men were of correct habits and that the agitation grew merely out of prejudice which had its beginning months before in an altercation which one of the teachers had with the editor of a local newspaper. On Saturday, the day set for their departure by the mass meeting at Boggy Swamp, the teachers had not obeyed the mandate of the committee. Another meeting was held, this time in the town of Kingstree, on the 26th. The afternoon train brought a number of interested persons. The conservative element was outnumbered, but prudence prevailed and the young men were allowed to remain to finish their term of work for which they had engaged, closing December 2 and 15 respectively. The committee remained in charge and reported in the local paper that they had seen one board the train the first of the month and without doubt the other must have decided to spend his Christmas holidays where the atmosphere was not so charged with iron.

It would be incorrect to imagine from all that has been said that the whole state was swept off its feet with excitement. In every community there was a conservative element that served to hold the agitation in check. Every community, however, appears to have had its fears aroused and the excitement in many parts was often at fever heat.

CHAPTER XVII. Prohibition of Educating the Negro

After seeing the situation in the South with reference to insurrections and the incendiarism of abolition, it will be easier to understand her attitude toward the education of the negro under the slavery regime. Most thinking people in the South today admit that the gradual education of the black is a positive good and that their fears of the effects from the most elementary teaching in former days was at least in large measure ill founded. On the other hand, getting their ante-bellum view and understanding their policy—probably lacking in progressive quality, but consistent—we are prepared to discuss the prohibition against instruction in reading and writing.

The act of 1740 imposed a fine of £100 upon any person teaching a slave to write. One of the reasons for such a prohibition may be inferred from the following quotation from an advertisement of a runaway in the City Gazette of July 11, 1805. The fact which it illustrates is applicable to slavery of any period of South Carolina history. "He [i. e., the runaway slave] is a tolerable good reader and writer; it is likely he will change his name, write himself a pass, and pass for a free man." Written permits to trade or for whiskey could very easily be used in the same way. It also made communication for insurrectionary purposes easy. Two negroes, who were brothers concerned in the Camden plot of 1816, it was shown could read and write. This prohibition seems tacitly to have been understood as not to apply to any master who desired his slaves to be taught—he being held apparently morally responsible by the community for the consequences—and at any rate they might be taught to read and taught such religious principles as should be thought desirable and necessary. McCrady mentions the existence of a negro school, near Charleston, where, through the efforts of the Society for the Propagation of the Gospel, a plantation was secured and slaves were bought for the purpose of being taught, chiefly religious training, with a view of sending them out as missionaries to other plantations. The school, beginning about 1743, enrolled at one time as many as seventy pupils. For about twenty years it was continued, but the lack of funds and probably the lack of the support of the community caused its discontinuance.

[An old negro of the writer's acquaintance boasts that he wrote passes not only for himself but for other slaves. The fact that scarcely one out of ten passes probably was ever called for by the holder's coming in contact with the patrol lends credence to the statement.]

As time went on the prohibition of instruction in writing was the only legal expression against negro education until 1834. Prior even to this, however, some doubt had been expressed as to the advisability of allowing them to be taught to read. Mention has already been made of the fact that some negroes concerned in the Camden and Charleston attempted uprisings could read and write. The Sumter grand jury in its presentment in 1829 took the following notice of it:

"The Grand Jury of Sumter District represent as a grievance of no inconsiderable degree, the liberty which is allowed to owners of teaching their slaves to read, a practice which if generally encouraged will lead to consequences of the most serious and alarming nature." Hon. Ed. R. Laurens, in another address before the Agricultural Society of South Carolina in 1832, complains that religious pressure is being brought too much to bear to educate slaves and adds that the law against slaves learning to write is a dead letter, for they are still permitted to learn to read.

The activity of the abolition agitation in the early thirties called forth probably the law of 1834 which forbade any white person on a penalty of a fine of $100 and six months' imprisonment to teach any slave to read or write. A free negro who should violate the provisions of the act was to be fined $50 and to receive fifty lashes. The slave who would undertake to teach slaves, not being capable of being reached by a fine, received the lashes. The reason for this attitude of the South is tritely and squarely put by Toombs, of Georgia:

"It is also objected that our slaves are debarred the benefit of any education. This objection is well taken and not without force; and for the evil the slaves are greatly indebted to the abolitionists. Formerly in some of the slaveholding states it was not forbidden to teach slaves to read and write; but the character of the literature sought to be furnished by the abolitionists caused the states to take counsel rather of their passions than of their reason, and to lay the axe at the root of the evil." The act of 1834 applied only to slaves. There seems to have been some effort to make a similar regulation for the free negroes or at least to prohibit negro schools, of which there must have been some at the time, as appears from a Charleston grand jury presentment in 1823:

"We present as a grievance the number of schools which are kept in the city by persons of color, and believe that a City Ordinance prohibiting, under severe penalties, such persons from being public instructors would meet with general approbation."

A more liberal policy, which characterized certainly a respectable minority of the whites, is to be seen from the following editorial utterance in the Charleston Courier of Dec. 9, 1835:

"The plan of prohibiting [i. e., by legislation—bills pending at the time] schools for free colored people strikes us as both unwise and inefficient. If public schools be prohibited the march of mind will yet progress under the domestic roof, and the effort to arrest it will prove worse than futile. Let these schools be rather regulated than prohibited and good may possibly be done—prohibit them and that will be done in secrecy which would not otherwise shun the light."

CHAPTER XVIII. Manumission

Until 1800 there was no restriction whatever placed by law upon the granting of freedom by a master to a slave as he might deem desirable or proper. It seems to have been regarded as a matter merely of individual preference. There had been, it is true, a colonial law as far back as 1722 requiring all owners who should set free any slave to provide for their departure from the province. But this act expired after a limited time as was the custom with colonial statutes and was not re-enacted. There were instances of slaves being freed by the colonial assembly as a reward for meritorious conduct.

The considerations that led to the imposing of restrictions is stated in the preamble to the act of 1800 as follows: "Whereas it has happened that many slaves of bad character or indigent or infirm have been set free." The act then went on to provide that any master desirous of manumitting any slave should appear with the slave before a magistrate and five freeholders, summoned by the magistrate for that purpose, prepared to answer all questions as to the slave's ability to earn his own living and as to his character. If the magistrates and freeholders should deem it advisable they might issue a certificate permitting the emancipation. This certificate was to be recorded by the clerk of court together with the deed of emancipation, a copy of which was to be made out by the clerk and given to the negro set free. Under this act any person might seize a negro set free thereafter in any other way, exception being made of those to whom a bequest of freedom had been previously made, and might appropriate the services of such negro to his own use. In 1831 a case was heard by the Court of Appeals involving the right of a negro to freedom, who had been allowed to act as a free man living on a farm to himself as early as 1800. The negro had been seized by an outsider under the provisions of this act. While the court did not confirm the title apparently acquired by the seizure it did declare that the negro was not a free man.

But emancipation came to involve further difficulties. There was a general feeling in the South that the free negro in large numbers, unrestricted by the restraining and controlling authority provided for in the slavery system, would be a great evil, a menace to the peace and welfare of the community. Wheeler, in his Law of Slavery, has the following note explanatory of the reasons for restraining emancipation:

"When it is considered that slaves are a peculiar species of property, it will not excite surprise that laws are necessary for their regulation and to protect society from even the benevolence of slaveowners, in throwing among the community a great number of stupid, ignorant, and vicious persons, to disturb its peace and to endanger its permanency.

"The right of society to regulate and control the ownership of this kind of property may be justified on the same grounds as some other species of property. No one can doubt the right of individuals to acquire, possess and sell gunpowder, but if the possessor chooses to take it to his house or store, in a city or populous town, the public becomes interested and will restrain him within reasonable and proper limits." Governor McDuffie expressed the feeling of his time in his annual message of 1835, using the following language:

"Emancipation would be a positive curse, depriving them of a guardianship essential to their happiness. . . . If emancipated where would they live? The idea of their remaining among us is utterly visionary. . . . The only disposition, therefore, that could be made of our emancipated slaves would be their transportation to Africa, to exterminate the native or be exterminated by them. . . . It is perfectly evident that the destiny of the negro race is either the worst possible form of political slavery, or domestic servitude as it exists in the slaveholding states." It would seem that this opinion of the prospective menace from the presence of the freed negroes in any very considerable numbers became more acute as time passed. The extreme picture of it is drawn by Hon. John Townsend in a speech at Charleston in 1860:

"It means again the turning loose upon society without the salutary restraints to which they are now accustomed more than four millions of a poor and very ignorant population to ramble in idleness over the country until their wants should drive most of them first to petty thefts and afterwards to the bolder crime of robbery and murder; or until their excesses, their impudence, their filth and starvation shall bring pestilence among them and sweep them off by thousands. Improvident to the last degree as they are, and accustomed to have all their wants attended to, day by day, would find them without provision; which night by night they must plunder of stock and of every other thing which they could carry off, until the country would be laid waste and impoverished by their interminable aggressions." This feeling of danger from the increase of the number of freedmen became so prevalent by 1820 that the legislature, in obedience to it, prohibited in that year the emancipation of any slaves, except by its own edict. At its next session in 1821 it had before it petitions from owners for permission to emancipate as many as forty-five slaves. A committee was appointed to investigate as to the desirability of complying with their prayers. It appears, however, that the failure of the legislature to take further action was intended to be interpreted that the law of 1820 was to be construed as an absolute prohibition except in unusual cases.

The most common circumstances under which emancipation of his slaves was sought by the master was in a will made often near the close of his life when in calmer moments he realized that some opportunity for bettering the condition of his slaves ought to be made possible; or when he desired to reward the faithfulness of a slave who perhaps was diligent in attending him in a last illness; or again he might wish to atone for some fancied or real cruelty to his slaves. After a life of self-interest had been served the man was more likely to be capable of looking at things in an unbiased light. But to leave a will to carry out such ideas involved his executors in difficulties from which they could not well escape. Realizing that peaceful emancipation could not be accomplished within the state, the testator often directed that they be removed from the state and set free. In 1835 the Court of Appeals held that this kind of will was not in violation of the letter or the spirit of the act of 1820, for it obviated the objection which that law sought to remove. This objection was that emancipation increased the number of free negroes in the community. But after removal and subsequent emancipation they could not return because of the prohibitions of the same law of 1820 against the immigration of free persons of color. This was directly in keeping with the sentiment expressed earlier by

Governor Geddes in 1820, the advice of whom with reference to the immigration of free negroes and emancipation was formulated into law just at that time. After speaking of the evil of the free negro immigrant he had said:

"The restrictions on emancipation might be dispensed with if persons emancipated should be obliged to depart the state, within a limited time, and not be allowed to return to it afterwards, without your authority, on pain of seizure. But lest such a condition annexed to emancipation should be deemed void, owners of slaves might be allowed to release all right to their service, provided they remove out of the state within a certain time, and their release to be in force during their absence from the state; and a slave to whom it may be given, to be liable to be seized as a slave on his being found within the state at any time after the period fixed by law for his leaving the same."

As already remarked the highest court seemed always to be very liberal in its interpretation of laws relating to slavery. This broad construction of the slave code was referred to as "judicial legislation" by a member of the general assembly in 1847 in the following words:

"Here is an illustration of judicial legislation. We have endeavored here to say, that no bequest of freedom to a slave shall take effect after the death of an owner . . . but the judges are opposed to this law and they are endeavoring by every mode to evade its operation." In 1840 there came up to the Court of Appeals the noted Carmille case. A slaveowner, Carmille, had died leaving a will which with reference to his slaves provided that they should be set free if possible. If they could not be legally emancipated they were to be conveyed in trust to certain trustees who would allow them to hire their time, paying only a nominal sum to the trustees.

This was unquestionably in conflict with the policy of the statutes on the subject of emancipation. Persons interested in the estate brought suit on the ground that the earnings of a slave belonged to his owner, in this case the heirs. The court held that the will of the testator was not contrary to the principles of the act of 1820 and was not in violation of the state's policy towards the negro, and that the will ought to be carried out.

This decision seems to have gone a step too far. It aroused the sentiment of the legislature and caused the passage of the sweeping act of 1841. This act shows that there were reasons other than the mere policy of preventing an increase in the number of free negroes in the state. It made void all bequests, deeds or trusts of slaves made with the stipulation that they be removed from the state and emancipated; it prohibited all gifts with secret or expressed understanding by which slaves should be removed from the state and set free; and provided that the donee might be held responsible to the heirs and next of kin for an accounting of the value of slaves so transferred by the donor; it nullified all bequests or trusts of slaves with a view of holding them in nominal slavery, but allowing them to act as free persons; it, also, prohibited any devise or bequest of property from being held in trust for the benefit of slaves. The statute depended for its due enforcement upon the provision that any person attempting to administer a will and carry out such provisions could be held financially responsible by heirs or other beneficiaries.

There was one point, however, while not so important, that the lawmakers overlooked, and the court in 1860 took occasion to uphold the validity of an emancipation where an owner himself took his slaves out of the state and set them free. In 1844 the court decided that the act of 1841 arrested the operation of a will made in 1839 that certain slaves should be removed from the state and emancipated by the executors of the estate of the deceased, since the will had not been carried out prior to the passage of the act, on the ground that no legal right can be vested in a slave. But in another case, in 1851, the court apparently reversed itself by declaring that a will allowing practical freedom, while nominal ownership was retained, was valid.

The act of 1841 was intended apparently to close every avenue of approach to emancipation. These laws are not always of course to be taken as a final indication of public sentiment. There was evidently a large class of persons who honestly desired to see a less severe policy pursued. Their views probably cannot be better expressed than in the clear and rugged style of Justice O'Neall. In 1845, he said:

"I think its policy [i. e., of the legislature against emancipation] so questionable that it ought to be repealed. A law, evaded as it is, and against which public sentiment, within and without the state, is so much arrayed, ought not to stand. It is better by far, that a wise and prudent system of emancipation, like that of 1800, should exist, rather than that unlicensed emancipation according to private arrangement should take place.

"What is there in the policy of the law of South Carolina to forbid emancipation by an owner, of a faithful, honest, good slave? Have we anything to fear from such a liberal and humane course. I should be sorry to believe that our domestic institution of slavery required any such restrictions upon the rights of the owners. Indeed, where anything is pushed to extremes injury is done to it; and that is now the case of the act of 1820 and other kindred provisions in other acts. They are continually thrust in our faces by those who undertook to meddle with matters which do not concern them, as evidence of our injustice and our sense of error in our slave system.

"Until fanaticism and folly drove us from that position the law of our state had uniformly favored emancipation by owners, of their slave property, with such limitations and guards as rendered the free negro not a dangerous, but a useful member of the community, however humble he might be. It is time we should return to it and say to all at home and abroad, we have nothing to fear from occasional emancipation."

While South Carolina cannot be set down as a community in which emancipation was often sought by masters for their slaves or that the small slaveholders or the nonslaveholding class very much desired increased opportunities for this class of the population, for they saw no other method of police control, still there were doubtless many evasions of the law and slaves were allowed to be de facto free. Heirs might claim their property but doubtless they often regarded the desire of the recently deceased relative. Or, if the slaves were allowed to go free in the lifetime of the owner, there was but little probability that they would ever be reduced to serfdom again. Judge O'Neal in his work on the Negro Law in South Carolina says of the laws against emancipation and their evasion:

"Like all of its class, it has done harm instead of good. It has caused evasions without number. These have been successful by vesting ownership in persons legally capable of holding it, and thus substantially conferring freedom, when it was legally denied." The instances of emancipation are necessarily to be thought of as comparatively few, probably fewer than the above quotation would seem to imply. The chief objection to the law prohibiting emancipation was in that it prevented all opportunity, or tended to prevent it, toward a peaceable and satisfactory gradual emancipation of those best fitted to exercise such freedom with broadest legal opportunity: however, it is probable that this would have made slower progress in South Carolina than in some other of the Southern states.

CHAPTER XIX. The Free Negro

It is probable that at an early period there were free negroes residing in the colony. It does not seem likely, however, that many came into the state in any other condition than as slaves. But doubtless setting them free came as a sort of careless use of the negro's services, or because he had in instances proved to be sufficiently useful to deserve reward. There were unquestionably a few free negroes in the colony when the first slave code of 1712 was framed; for the latter, in section 1, defines as slaves all who were then held as such or who should hereafter be sold or bought, except those who could prove that they ought not to be held in slavery. Less than ten years prior to the Revolution the Charleston grand jury had the following to say of them:

"We present as a grievance, the bad practice of free negroes and mulattoes being suffered to pass to and fro without any certificate or badge of their being free, by which means many runaway slaves are suffered to pass as free."

The first legislation dealing specifically with the free negro as distinguished from the slave was passed in 1794 and prohibited the immigration of free negroes into the state and directed that any so offending should be transported whence they came. This was renewed in 1800 by an act which also prohibited the introduction of slaves from other states.

For a long time the free negro was a sort of non-descript so far as his status legally and socially was concerned. But after some time the control of this class of persons not subject to the slavery system gave concern. Their number had gone on increasing by additional emancipations from year to year. In 1790 there were 1,801 free negroes in the state, 3,185 in 1800, in 1820 6,826, in 1860 9,914.

The whites usually looked upon the possibilities of the free negro's situation for insurrectionary purposes as being very great. Hence on November 30, 1819, the house of representatives adopted, in committee of the whole, the following resolution :

"That it is expedient to prohibit the further introduction of free negroes in this state."

It was in 1820 that the general assembly prohibited any further emancipation. This was part of a definite policy of the state to prevent, as far as possible, any increase in the number of this variety of the population. As a companion piece of legislation there was another provision embraced in the same act to prohibit the immigration of free negroes into the state. Any free negro entering the state from the outside was to be arrested and taken before a magistrate who was to direct him to leave the state and in case he failed to do so within fifteen days he was to be fined $20, a process which could be repeated indefinitely. It is not probable that many free negroes came. Gov. Geddes had said in his message of 1820:

"In connection, however, with this subject, I deem it proper to inform you that a number of free persons of color have emigrated and are daily emigrating to and settling in this stale. The policy of our country forbids the increase of this class of persons among us, and under existing circumstances imperatively calls for the adoption of the strongest measures to prevent it, and it may be deemed a duty to oppose at the threshold everything likely in its consequences to disturb our domestic tranquility." But what seems to have had more influence on the legislators is thus told in the legislative news items in the Charleston Courier of December 12, 1820:

"Three interesting papers from an unknown writer under the signature of a 'Carolinian' were laid on the desk of the members of the State legislature a few days since . . . reprobating in bold and energetic language the evil policy of continuing to admit in such numbers, free persons of color to settle amongst us. . . . The statements and parts detailed in these papers had excited much attention at Columbia." We have already called attention to the profound impression that was made by the Vesey plot in Charleston. The only legislative acts that can be cited as due entirely to this excitement were those made with a view to the further restriction of the free negro. The seamen acts, already referred to, were passed to prevent any pernicious activity of any free negroes who were members of the crews of visiting sea-going vessels. Every free negro, from fifteen to fifty years old, if he was not a native of the state or had not been a resident of the state for five years, was made by this act, liable to an annual tax of $50. This same act provided that every free male negro over fifteen years of age should have a guardian who in law was a "next friend" or "prochein ami." This guardian was to be "a respectable freeholder" of the district in which the negro lived. It should be his duty in becoming the guardian of this ward to go before the clerk of court of that district, giving his certificate that the negro in question "is of good character and correct habits," and then to signify in another signed statement his acceptance of the guardianship of said negro. Any free negro failing to provide himself with the necessary legal guardian was to be treated as a free negro entering the state.

In the Sumter clerk of court's office is to be found an old record book, the first of its kind evidently for that district, for the act of 1822 was the first of such enactments; the book has the title "Guardians of Free Negroes." This particular book covers the years 1823-1842. In 1823, when the law first went into effect, there are twenty guardianships recorded. The largest number recorded after this is five in 1840, there being none recorded in some years. In another book in the same office are to be found lists of children of free negroes certified to by the guardian.

The guardian was to be to the free negro what the master was to the slave. This was the result of the effort to require every free negro to have some white person who would vouch for, or be responsible for, the negro. The extent of this responsibility was not great except in legal actions. There is every reason, however, to believe that any white person who took a sufficiently kindly interest in a free colored man was a source of protection to him. Advice as to his business affairs, attention in illness, or reproof for misconduct would naturally be supposed to be the proper services rendered such a colored ward by his guardian. The quasi-authority of the guardian could probably be enforced by a threat to withdraw his guardianship; though the law does not indicate whether this could be withdrawn at will or not. It was not intended that the guardian should in any way limit the freedom of the negro to move about from place to place, or to trade or to hire himself. By the act of 1835 the free person of color was forbidden to carry arms except with a written permit from his guardian.

It would be interesting to know how, when this act was passed in 1822, the body of negroes then free secured protection of the necessary guardian. But if they were agreeable, honest and orderly they probably found no great difficulty in acquiring a guardian among the families of their former owners or employers. He may in some instances have even rendered slight services. There would be every reason to believe that free negro men often grew up without such legal formal acceptance of a guardianship by a white person. But if any occasion arose which legally necessitated a guardian, as for example the collection of a debt due the negro, the white person could be found who would accept. There was no law holding the guardian in any way financially or otherwise responsible for the conduct of his ward. There was likely, however, pressure of public sentiment in that direction.

The legal status of the free person of color may now be described in substance. He was tried for crime before the same kind of court as that provided for the trial of slaves; he was subject to the same kind of penalties—corporal punishment—with the possible addition of a fine; his testimony could not be accepted in court against a white person, though a slave was a competent witness against a free negro; he had full right to acquire, hold and transfer property; he might and did often own slaves. The right of free negroes to hold property, particularly property in slaves, was thus defended by the Charleston Courier of December 8, 1835:

"The projected denial of the right of slave ownership [debated in the legislature] is another measure of obviously mistaken policy. His right to hold slaves gives him a stake in the institution of slavery and makes it his interest as well as his duty to uphold it. It identifies his interests and his feelings in this particular with those of the white population, and we can imagine no sufficient reason for the severance. The hardship, too, of the case is worth consideration—the right has not only been enjoyed for years but in many cases since the enactment of our law against manumission it has been the only means of placing husband and wife under one roof and in the bosom of one family—and we cannot relish the idea of compelling the husband to sell his wife or the parent the child." The best authoritative statement of the legal status, rights and privileges of the free negro may be found in the Harden case coming up to the Court of Appeals in 1832 from Chester district. A free negro, according to the testimony of other white men, had been unmercifully and without cause beaten by a white man. The case reached the highest court on the objection that an indictment for assault upon a negro could not lie.

The important part of the decision is as follows:

"Free negroes without any of the political rights that belong to a citizen are still, to some extent, regarded by the law as possessing both natural and civil rights. The rights of liberty, life and property belong to them and must be protected by the community in which they are suffered to live. They are regarded, in law, as persons capable of committing or receiving an injury; and for the one they are liable for punishment, and for the other they are entitled to redress."

"For to no white man does the right belong of correcting at pleasure a free negro. The peace of society is as much broken by an assault upon him as it is upon a white man. Like the latter, he has his passions, and with the means of attack and defense in his possession, if the law refused to protect him, he, too, at last, might be driven to repel force by force. The only difference in the law as to indictments for assaults and batteries on free white men and free negroes, seems to me to consist in the different justification which would excuse an assault and battery on the one or the other. Free negroes belong to a degraded caste of society; they are in no respect on an equality with a white man. According to their condition they ought by law to be compelled to demean themselves as inferiors, from whom submission and respect to the whites, in all their intercourse in society, is demanded; I have always thought and while on the circuit ruled that words of impertinence and insolence, addressed by a free negro to a white man, would justify an assault and battery."

The free negroes as individuals very probably always had friends, but as a class they were often distrusted by the whites and scorned by the slaves. To the well-kept house slave, the phrase "no 'count as a free nigger" was the bitterest reproach that could be cast upon him by his fellows or his master. Perhaps one of the most reliable statements with reference to his standing in the community is to be found as an incidental remark in the case of Vinyard vs. Passalaigne, decided in 1845:

"Everyone knows, that the free negroes in South Carolina are far, very far, from being a class envied by our slaves. Generally they are worse off in every respect; they throw themselves under the sheltering wing of some benevolent white man, and instead of being fomenters of insubordination and rebellion among slaves, they pursue here a directly contrary course." A favorable estimate of the condition and character of the free negro can be seen in an editorial in the Charleston Courier of December 9, 1835:

"We are free, too, to confess that the conduct of the free colored people of this city, if not of the state, has been for the most part so correct, evincing so much civility, subordination, industry and propriety, that unless their conduct should change for the worse, or some stern necessity demand it, we are unwilling to see them deprived of those immunities which they have enjoyed for centuries without the slightest detriment to the commonwealth." Weston, writing in 1857, expresses doubt as to the free negro being so profligate as is often charged because the fact that their numbers are uniformly maintained would seem to indicate the opposite.

There was a general tendency to discriminate against the free negro. In Marion no free person of color was allowed to follow regular employment without a permit, granted upon the payment of a fee of $1.50. Charleston laid a tax of $10 on free negro males from twenty-one to sixty years of age "who are carrying on any trade or art or being a mechanic." E. R. Laurens found the opposition, particularly in Charleston, to the free negro to be in the fact that he competed to some extent in the skilled trades. In 1848 by the industrial census of the city of Charleston we find with reference to free negroes that there were 42 tailors and cap makers, 27 carpenters and joiners, 17 boot and shoe makers, and 196 colored free women as seamstresses and mantuamakers—more than all other seamstresses combined.

Free negro males from eighteen to fifty years of age were subjected to a poll tax of two dollars, for failure to pay which the sheriff was authorized to sell him for a period of service not more than five years, sufficient to pay the costs.

While competition with the white laboring class might cause dissatisfaction with the free negro of Charleston, where about eight per cent, of the colored population was free, it does not appear that the hostility to the free negro was any more bitter in Charleston, if as bitter, than it was in other parts of the state. It was from other parts of the state, where farming and cotton raising chiefly was the principal industry, and hence where there was practically no competition offered by them, and where the free negroes were fewer in number, that a most unfriendly feeling toward them existed. The case was coldly summed up in a letter by R. G. Harper in the First Annual Report of the Colonization Society. His view was that the free negro is inferior socially, improvident, liable to corrupt and poison the minds of the slaves who envy his condition, works occasionally, assists slaves in theft, becoming thus a medium for illegal trading, affords opportunity for unlawful meetings and insurrectionary movements. This view can be compared with that of a "Carolinian," who thinks that mulattoes form a sort of barrier between the slave and white acting as a preventive of insurrections.

We have already quoted some of the more favorable opinions concerning the free negroes. It will now be appropriate to give a few extracts typical of the unfavorable estimate of them as a class. The latter form the larger part of the contemporary comments on this subject. Here may be quoted a mild editorial accusation against this class from the Camden Journal of November 19, 1850:

"The free negroes as a class are the most miserable set of creatures upon earth; having the right of property in our midst, besides enjoying many privileges which our slaves do not have, they possess the means of corrupting, and do corrupt and destroy in a moral and physical sense, the actual value of that species of property which is the source and cause of so much strife in the Federal Government, and which is likely to involve us in a second Revolution." The newspaper comments on the free person of color have the ring of prejudice and insincerity about them. While the free negro was amenable to the magistrates' court still the grand jury of Marlborough district in 1850 took cognizance of the rather obstreperous conduct of a certain free negro in that community using the following language: "We present that James Young, a Free Negro, is in the habit of carrying concealed deadly weapons, and has made threat to take the life of Gilbert Oxendinel, also a free negro, and we pray the court to take such measures as will bring the said Young to Summary justice."

Another more biased illustration of the newspaper talk will suffice. The editorial management of the Rising Sun of Newberry developed an extremely strong dislike for this species of the population. In an editorial of May 19, 1858, some of the things complained of are: renting of houses to free negroes, thus becoming a rendezvous for crime— "Brothels, greasy spots. Black Marks"; hiring to them horses and buggies; permitting them to career around to the envy of the slaves; collecting of negroes on public corners and places in the town; he winds up with, "Oh, vi et armis per cowhide." The editor in 1860 became a candidate for the legislature and one of the planks of his platform was to require each free negro to choose a master and re-enter slavery. He was not elected but probably this idea of his lost him no votes. This same feeling, whether with good reason or not, was shared by the grand jury of Union district in 1855. It said:

"We further present as a public nuisance the fact that a number of worthless free negroes harbor in and around this village without any visible means of support."

To the writer the picture of the free negro as it is here given appears for the following reasons to be somewhat overdrawn: First, the comments are usually generalizations, with but few specific charges and rarely is an individual case cited to illustrate the charge. Unfortunately no records of the courts for the trial of slaves and free negroes were kept. Hence what would give us the best clue as to the number of criminals and the frequency of crime among the free negroes is not available. Secondly, in contrast with these comments unfavorable to the free negroes stands other evidence, typical extracts of which were quoted, that gives the free negroes a reputation for orderliness and thrift. Some of this evidence, too, is from sources the most reliable and least likely to be biased. Thirdly, the recollections of survivors of the ante-bellum period substantiate this favorable opinion of the free negroes as a class. This kind of evidence, while the weakest critically however, is worth considering as corroborative testimony. The writer has talked with numbers of the older citizens of the state and in reply to specific inquiries they almost uniformly remember the free negroes, as persons who rarely caused disturbance of the peace or became by their shiftlessness a charge to the community. Fourthly, many of the unfavorable opinions, particularly the editorial comments of newspapers in the extravagance of their statement, often betray a tone of prejudice and insincerity. Whether the free negroes were the serious menace to the peace and welfare of the community that they are frequently represented to have been may be doubted. But the readiness of the whites to charge any disorderly conduct among the negroes to the agency of the colored freemen must have operated as a check upon them, since it is reasonable to believe that they were aware of this suspicious concern with which the superior race watched their conduct. This hostility to the colored freeman began to crystallize into a definitely expressed policy. One of the plans of dealing with the free negro was deportation. "The Southern Rights Association," of Kershaw district, as early as 1850, took the following action:

"Resolved that the Chairman of the several Committees of safety constitute a committee to circulate memorials to the Legislature of this State to provide the means for removing from her borders all free persons of color." Governor Seabrook, in his annual message of 1850, bowing to the popular bias, had the following to say of the character of the free negro and how to deal with him:

"Although the mind of the community has not been prepared by public discussion or perhaps by private interchange of views on the subject, yet it is my deliberate opinion that the period has arrived for the removal from the State of every free colored person who is not the owner of real estate or slave property. This population is not only a non-productive class, but it is, and always has been, essentially corrupt and corrupting. Their longer residence among us, if the warfare between the North and South is to continue, will eventually generate evils difficult of eradication. Possessing, in an unlimited degree, the right of locomotion, they can in person bear intelligence in a day, from one section of a State to another, or through the post office mature their own plans of villainy, as well as execute orders emanating from foreign sources. There is, indeed, too much reason to believe, that at this moment they are made to occupy the situation of spies in our camp, and to disseminate through the entire body of our slave population the poison of insubordination, prepared in the great northern laboratory of fanaticism." The part of the governor's message recommending deportation was referred to the committee on the colored population. Its report was unfavorable to the scheme. Its impracticability is summed up by the committee in somewhat the following way : the plan is novel and has not been under discussion by the people; it would recognize the principles of the colonization societies not favored in South

Carolina; it would work an undue hardship on the free negroes and particularly in a property way; the expense is considerable—would it be paid out of confiscation of the free negro's property or state funds? If in the latter way it would prove too great a burden; it would put the state in a bad light in the eyes of the world. The problem they suggested in dealing with the idle and dissolute freeman of color they say "can be met with judicious penal legislation sufficient to repress the evil without resorting to the extreme measure indicated by his Excellency." Nothing further in a legislative way seems to have come of the plan.

This recommendation of the governor seems to have been somewhat premature and not much more appears to have been said with reference to it until near the close of the decade. In the fall of 1858 the grand jury of York district in its presentment recommended that the state appropriate sufficient funds for the removal of the free negroes to Liberia, giving those who desired to remain the alternative of choosing a master and becoming a slave. And at the same term of the court at Union the grand jury said of them:

"To strengthen our peculiar Institution (slavery) and to remove a source of competition from among our slaves, we recommend the passing of a law to clear the State of all free persons of colour."

In the following spring the Williamsburg grand jury of a district having only thirty-seven free negroes by the census of 1850 had this to say of this questionable class:

"We further present the free negroes of the district as a nuisance and recommend that the Legislature pass some law that will have the effect of relieving the community of this troublesome population."

At the spring term of the Newberry court, the grand jury made recommendations as to the disposal of the free persons of color similar to that made in York the preceding fall.

The excitement after the Brown raid in Virginia has already been referred to; the feeling vented itself largely on the free negro. He was looked upon as the most likely point and source of trouble. The general assembly became the forum for a part of the discussion for a solution of the apparent danger. To the old idea of transportation in 1850 was added that of re-enslavement referred to in the two grand jury presentments quoted above. One plan was transportation with re-enslavement as the alternative; another was to make enslavement the penalty for crimes not now capital for free negroes; still another was complete and entire re-enslavement, allowing the colored freeman to choose his master, while some desired them all to be sold indiscriminately. Bills embodying all of these different views were introduced but nothing further than discussion came of them. Old negroes of that day who are still living recall the talk of this time about re-enslaving the free negro and feel now that this agitation was taken advantage of by the white man to hold it over the head of the colored freeman as a threat.

There was a general feeling prevalent that the free negro was an anomaly, that he prevented the homogeneity of slavery as an industrial institution or system of paternal control. He was neither citizen nor dependent of the state. This was at least one reason for the agitation. The slave owner felt him as a competitive producer. The class of non-slaveholding whites assisted in maintaining the system of slavery for they felt that there was no other adequate system of controlling this heterogeneous mass of racially degraded class of the population; naturally they felt that the colored freeman did not come under this controlling power and was a menace to the welfare and peace of the community.

To this must be added the agitation of the slavery question by outsiders which provoked the people into statements not accurately representative of the feeling of the people at large or the general public sentiment.

170

CONCLUSION

One of the striking things about slavery in South Carolina was the conservatism of the superior race toward any substantial modification of the institution. Amended, of course, from time to time, the code of 1740 remained for one hundred and twenty years the organic slave law of the state. However, the system of slavery, which was crude in its beginnings, slowly underwent changes that marked its development and gave to it a fixed form as a social and economic organization. A good illustration of this growth is the evolution of the patrol. Many of these modifications both in legal enactment and practical operation were in the direction of an amelioration of the condition of the blacks: kidnapping of free negroes, at first not prohibited, was later made a crime; the murder of a negro by a white person, which until 1821 was punishable only by a fine and imprisonment, was after that made a capital offense; the court for the trial of negroes was modified so as to prevent some of the glaring injustice of the earlier procedure; privileges of trading and hiring their time were legally denied to slaves, but as time went on apparently the violations of these laws became more common and were passed unnoticed. On the other hand some of the changes, in so far as granting the inferior race advantage were concerned, were reactionary: manumission, unrestricted until 1800, had after that to be brought about by legal permission, and was prohibited entirely in 1820; strictures on the free negroes prohibiting their entrance into the state and even proposing their re-enslavement became more marked as time went on; at first the whites were forbidden to teach slaves to write, and later as the result of the abolition movement they were also forbidden to teach them to read.

The explanation of this conservatism is to be found chiefly in the need of an adequate police control for the inferior race which slavery provided. The financial interests of the large planters are sufficient to explain why they sought to perpetuate such a system of labor. But why should the non-slaveholders, who formed the majority of the white population, have assisted in upholding and maintaining the slavery status of the negro with its attendant inconveniences, such as patrol service, when they must have been aware in some measure at least that as an economic regime it was a hindrance to their progress? Was it not because they felt that their personal security and that of their families depended upon an arrangement which gave the superior race a means of control that they imagined could not be evolved with the inferior race living under any other status? The horror inspired by the possibility of any great number of unattached negroes found expression in the newspaper criticisms of the conduct of the free negroes.

In this study of South Carolina slavery the writer has found nothing to indicate that there was any movement or any serious discussion of the advisability of abolishing slavery or devising any plan that would eventually lead to it. Apparently no anti-slavery leaders like those in Virginia or North Carolina ever flourished in South Carolina. The Quakers, who were opposed to slavery, left the state in the early part of the nineteenth century, or gave up their scruples about it. The German settlers in Orangeburg and Lexington districts sought to abstain from slavery but drifted with the current and became slaveholders. Some doubtless deprecated slavery in an academic way, and some even maintained in practice their belief that slavery was wrong. Whether there was no tendency toward agitation or public sentiment suppressed it, would be difficult to determine. There is little reason to believe that such discussion would have secured an intelligent hearing.

There was a decided tendency on the part of the benevolently disposed before 1830 to better the condition of the negroes by religious teaching and by encouraging the owners to allow them such privileges as would be consistent with their relation to the whites. Some, like Judge O'Neall, favored an opportunity being allowed for the emancipation of exceptionally worthy slaves. But the abolition interference from the outside checked every movement that had any suggestion of progress in this direction, and set a social stigma and legal punishment upon him who was so imprudent as to call in question any feature of the characteristically Southern institution.

It is not to be inferred that if there had been no outside meddling South Carolina shivery would have been very much modified. The presumption is decidedly the other way, for the slave had not become less valuable to the slaveholder toward the close of the slavery period, as was the case in Virginia and North Carolina. In most respects South Carolina was at one with the gulf states in her attitude toward slavery and her policy in controlling the inferior race, as well as in her financial interest in slavery.

Something has already been said as to the distribution of the slaves over the state. Slavery conditions in the uplands were not the same as in the lowlands. In the former the prevailing rule was a small farm with few slaves, the owner usually living on the farm with his slaves, and the white population in the community outnumbered the blacks. In the lowlands the large plantation with many negroes under an overseer and few whites was the type. Possibly, then, South Carolina represented practically every variety of condition in which negroes lived in the South. Again it will be seen that Charleston afforded a most interesting variety of conditions under which the Carolina negro lived. The free negro, the slave who was allowed to hire his time, the slave under partial restriction, the slave under complete oversight of the master—each of these classes was represented. It is to be admitted that Charleston was not entirely successful in the control of these classes but afforded a curious combination of progressiveness and conservatism from which either those who desired further restrictions or those who advocated a more liberal policy, could draw illustrations.

9 781678 057657